A Brief History of
Fort Washington, Pennsylvania

A Brief History of
Fort Washington, Pennsylvania

From Farmland to Suburb

Lewis and Trudy Keen

Charleston   London

History
PRESS

Published by The History Press
Charleston, SC 29403
www.historypress.net

Cover Image: Camp Hill Hall, built in 1882 by John and Sarah Drexel Fell, was one of the earliest and most important estates in the Fort Washington Area. *Photo courtesy of Drexel Archives.*

First published 2006

Manufactured in the United Kingdom

ISBN 1.59629.127.3

Keen, Lewis.
 A brief history of Fort Washington, Pennsylvania : from farmland to suburb
/ Lewis and Trudy Keen.
 p. cm.
 Includes bibliographical references and index.
 ISBN 1-59629-127-3 (alk. paper)
 1. Fort Washington (Pa.)--History. 2. Fort Washington
(Pa.)--History--Pictorial works. 3. Historic buildings--Pennsylvania--Fort
Washington. 4. Fort Washington (Pa.)--Buildings, structures, etc. 5. Real
estate development--Pennsylvania--Fort Washington--History. I. Keen, Trudy.
II. Title.
 F159.F695K44 2006
 974.8'12--dc22
                                     2006009751

CONTENTS

ACKNOWLEDGEMENTS

This book was created with the assistance of numerous individuals and organizations. Betty Sadler, William "Buck" Amey, Nick Guilbert, Ingrid Rivel, Tom Rivel and Robin Costa are fellow local historians from the Historical Society of Fort Washington who supported and aided this endeavor with their knowledge and enthusiasm. Additional local historians gracious enough to share information and photographs with us included Ralph and Pam Jennings, the late Newton Howard and Edward T. Addison Jr. The living legends in the neighborhood, George Haggar, Helen Klosterman Jensen, Gloria Mallozzi and Janice Klosterman, shared with us their memories and love for this special place we call the Heights. This project would never have made it to the printed page without the suggestions and support of Marcia Dunn.

We are also grateful to Timothy Illingworth, Frank and Linda King, Helga and Jennie Woodword, Beatrice Bodenstein, Hellen Kuleskey, John R. Fell III, Bob Hibbert, Grace Earwaker, Anna and Herbert Miller, Lesterle Meyer, Nan Warren, Robert and Gladys Buck, David Negley and Ted and Martha Gay for their contributions.

The staff at the Historical Society of Montgomery County kindly responded to all requests, usually involving armloads of tax books being carried in and out in less than desirable weather conditions. A special thank you to Jeff McGranahan.

Thanks to the staff at Recorder of Deeds Office, Norristown, Pennsylvania, for their assistance in "pulling" film for us in a timely and professional manner.

The Friends of Mather Mill, Friends of Hope Lodge, Drexel University Archives, Bruce Laverty and the Athenaeum of Philadelphia, William Patterson of the Philadelphia Sketch Club also provided needed information for this book. The Historical Society of Fort Washington remains the starting place for anyone doing local research. For seventy years it has protected the stories about the history of this area and continues to do so today.

INTRODUCTION

The name Fort Washington was first used by the North Pennsylvania Railroad to identify its station, which opened here in 1855. They chose this name because of the earthen redoubt used by Washington's troops during the 1777 Whitemarsh Encampment. Prior to the arrival of the railroad, the southern section of Fort Washington was called Whitemarsh, and the northern part was referred to as Pinetown. Over the years many authors and researchers have documented the Revolutionary War time period of the region. Accounts of local history would lead readers to believe that nothing happened after Washington's troops left the area until major highway construction took place in the twentieth century. As a result, the events from the late nineteenth and early twentieth centuries in Fort Washington have been largely overlooked. This time period was one of incredible change in the area as well as in the nation. The focus of this book is to document this significant time period in Fort Washington and specifically a section referred to as the Heights.

Documents concerning eighteenth century buildings in the suburban Philadelphia vicinity are plentiful and provided ample information for this text. However, few documents have been published that describe the events that transformed the community from farmland to suburb, and the oldest of citizens today have few or no memories before the 1930s. These circumstances indicate the importance of the *Ambler Gazette* in documenting this time period in Fort Washington. Each week the *Gazette* published the stories of the wealthy as well as those about ordinary citizens. The *Gazette* covered the news in a section much more extensive than the borough of Ambler. Each week its reporters covered seven townships and almost thirty communities.

In 1995 we purchased a Queen Anne house on Summit Avenue in Fort Washington. After a few years of researching the history of the house, our interest broadened to include other houses in the neighborhood. Then we realized that in order to complete the picture of history in this area, we needed to look at the buildings, businesses and people along Bethlehem Pike. Each week the *Ambler Gazette* carried a column called "Fort Washington," which provided us with the geographical parameters for our research. This book does not cover the entire locale we know today as Fort Washington. We chose to focus on the fifty-year time period from roughly 1875–1925 because that was when the majority of important changes took place. The book includes a brief narrative of the history of Fort Washington as well as an inventory of existing, original structures for the Heights.

Determining the date of construction of a house can be a daunting task. By using a combination of deeds, county tax records, maps and information from *Ambler Gazette*s, we were able to date most of the houses in the Heights. In cases where the sources disagreed and we were unable to pinpoint a construction date, we included the information for readers to review. In some cases the completion date could be the year previous to the date listed, but items in the *Ambler Gazette* confirmed many of the dates we list. Since the inventory includes more than one hundred properties, errors may have occurred, but we have made every effort to supply dates about which we were confident.

Every town has its local legends, and Fort Washington is no exception. One of the prevalent stories involves 301–303 Summit Avenue, a Queen Anne twin. At some point someone began to tell the story of the two sisters. The man who had the house built, a judge in Norristown, had two daughters. He wanted each of them to have the luxury of a house, but he knew they wanted to remain close to each other. So he built the twin with connecting doors on all three floors. Although the story was intriguing, never at any time were the houses inhabited by sisters, and connecting doors were never found. A man known as the Judge did reside at 303 Summit Avenue in the 1920s, but he was actually a probation officer. Part of the confusion may have begun because a house on Fort Washington Avenue built for family members did have doors to connect the two halves. From this experience we learned that researchers can't believe everything they hear. We also realized that just because someone owned a property doesn't necessarily mean he lived at that address. Often in Fort Washington people bought speculative houses or rental properties. We used to assume that a one-dollar sale meant the people involved in the sale were related, but at times the transaction involved a mortgage of a hefty sum separate from the sale. Finally, early federal censuses don't involve house numbers, so researchers must rely on parcel numbers and deeds.

The *Gazette* traces its beginning to 1883. There is a notation in *Montgomery County: The Second Hundred Years* that the paper started as the *Fort Washington Times* and was published from 1879 to 1882. Records indicate that from 1882 the *Ambler Times* was published weekly by Dr. Rhoades and was followed by the *Ambler Gazette*, published by Horace G. Lukens, in 1883. Historians claim that local news accounted for a small percentage of the early edition of the paper, but since none are known to exist, the story is impossible to confirm. Before 1896, the paper was purchased by A.K. Thomas of Lansdale. During that time the office was first located at Race and Main Street in Ambler and later moved to 49 East Butler Avenue. The office burned but was rebuilt and remained at this location until 1981. The paper moved additional times and had many publishers. William E. Strasburg served as publisher from 1952 until 1989. The paper published about eight pages each week from the earliest papers presently known to exist (1897) until 1948. From that year forward, the number of pages increased significantly to about fifty-five each week. The paper has been continuously published since 1883.

Only one collection of *Ambler Gazette*s is known to be in existence today and is housed at the Historical Society of Fort Washington. The collection is not in climate-controlled conditions and is deteriorating. These papers are used by local historians and provide invaluable information for the research of this time period of Fort Washington. Two copies of microfilm created in the 1970s of the papers are in use today, but they are also in poor condition. Efforts are underway to microfilm the collection, digitize it and make it available on the Internet for all to use. Profits from this book will be used to help fund the project.

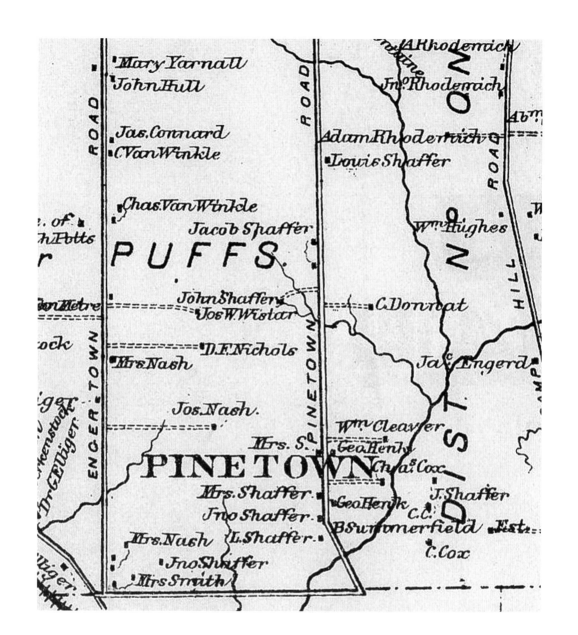

This 1877 map shows that, prior to development, the area of Fort Washington in Upper Dublin Township was known as Pinetown. *Courtesy of Historical Society of Fort Washington.*

THE EARLY YEARS
FARMLAND AND POST-RAILROAD DEVELOPMENT

Fort Washington consists of what were two land grants from William Penn. The land located in Whitemarsh Township was part of the land granted to Major Jasper Farmar, and the Upper Dublin part was granted to Edward Tanner. Major Jasper Farmar, a British army officer from Cork, Ireland, died before arriving here. His land was settled by his widow and children by 1685. The early development occurred along what is currently Bethlehem Pike, which was a cart way as early as 1698 and developed into an important road by 1714. In the Whitemarsh section, houses and businesses, such as inns and taverns, were built as a result of traffic along the road. The presence of streams in the area encouraged the building of mills. During the same time period, a part of Fort Washington that lies in Upper Dublin Township was farmland but later developed into the residential neighborhood known as Fort Washington Heights.

John Tanner sold land in 1681 to John Potts, who sold some of his land to Peter Cleaver in 1721. Cleaver farmed one hundred acres along Fort Washington Avenue and built his house at 113 Fort Washington Avenue in 1752. The Window Pane Tax of 1798 indicates other early farmers were John Everhat (Everhard), John Colar (Coler) and Jacob Slauter. By 1855 Daniel Nash had purchased much of the land in Fort Washington Heights and continued using it for farmland. That same year the North Pennsylvania Railroad extended its line through Fort Washington. While the purpose of the railroad line was to bring coal from the Lehigh Valley to Philadelphia, its impact on the area was more far-reaching. The area had long been a refuge for people to escape the heat of the city, and train service made the trip easier. Soon people realized Fort Washington provided a lovely place to live year-round and required just a short train ride to the city. A suburb was born!

The development of Fort Washington Heights began in the 1870s when Joseph Rex laid out lots of land to be sold for William Whitall of Philadelphia. By 1873, Whitall had sold at least some land to Henry Bissinger of Philadelphia. Bissinger sold land to Edwin Arnold of Philadelphia in 1877. Arnold had Charles K. Aiman resurvey the land; Fort Washington Avenue, Pennsylvania Avenue, Madison Avenue and Spring Avenue roughly

CHAS. K. AIMAN,
Co. Surveyor.

Joseph Hunter, who surveyed the Cummings land for the Heights. *Courtesy of Historical Society of Fort Washington.*

Charles K. Aiman, who surveyed the Arnold land for the Heights. *Courtesy of Historical Society of Fort Washington.*

An 1886 plot plan, done by Charles K. Aiman for Edwin Arnold, shows the potential development of the Heights. *Courtesy of Historical Society of Fort Washington.*

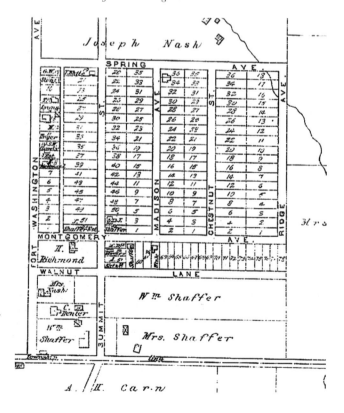

bordered this area. The Arnold development accounts for the largest number of houses built in this part of the neighborhood.

In 1879, Henry Bissinger bought land from Daniel Nash. He was unable to meet his debts, and the land reverted to Nash through the sheriff. The second wave of development in the Heights began when farmer Joseph Nash, son of Daniel Nash, sold about forty-two acres of land to George Cummings of Philadelphia in 1886. The Cummings acreage was surveyed by Joseph Hunter and was roughly bordered by Spring Avenue, Hartranft Avenue, Fort Washington Avenue and Madison Avenue. Hartranft Avenue originally started at Fort Washington Avenue and ended at Madison Avenue.

The advent of railroad service had a significant impact on Fort Washington. Industries that could receive materials and export their finished product more easily were attracted to the area. One early endeavor was the Flues Silk Mill on Morris Road just above Bethlehem Pike. The mill was established near the Heights on the site of a former gristmill by a firm of New York commission merchants that included Charles Hieronius, Eberhard Flues and Charles Spielman. Under the name of Flues and Company, the mill operated from 1867 until 1874. For much of its history, it was a worsted mill that made fringed shawls, which were very fashionable in that time period. At its peak the mill was operating twenty looms and employing over one hundred people. A more complete account of mills in the region can be found in Dr. Mary Hough's *An Early History of Ambler*.

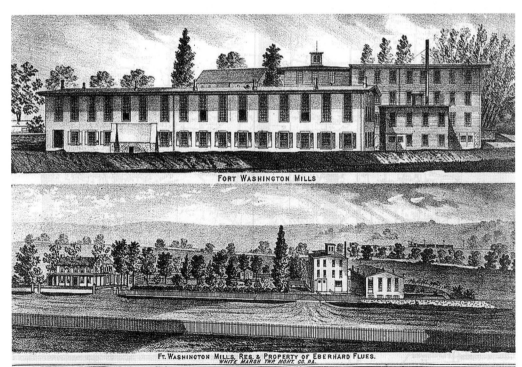

FORT WASHINGTON MILLS

FT. WASHINGTON MILLS, RES. & PROPERTY OF EBERHARD FLUES.
WHITE MARSH TWP. MONT. CO. PA.

The Flues Silk Mill was along the Wissahickon Creek between Bethlehem Pike and Butler Avenue. *Courtesy of Historical Society of Montgomery County.*

Just after the turn of the century, Hoopes and Townsend opened a rolling mill to manufacture steel for their bolt making business in the city. The section around the mill, known as Hoopeston, was a typical industrial company town that included housing for the workers, a company store and the factory. The *Gazette* carried a paragraph in January of 1901 that Hoopes and Townsend had made a survey of Hoopeston and Fort Washington. The rumor in the village was that they planned to incorporate the two places and do away with the historic name of Fort Washington. A meeting was held at the home of A.H. Carn to see just how far matters had progressed. Of course nothing ever came of the residents' fears. In 1907 the mill began making horseshoe iron and steel tires. In 1917 a rumor surfaced that the mill was to be purchased by Bethlehem Steel, but by 1925 the mill closed and it was torn down by 1928. The swampy conditions around the mill town and the air pollution caused by the mill made this area much less healthy than the office park that now occupies this land.

Hoopes and Townsend, manufacturers of bolts and screws, was founded by Barton Hoopes, Edward Hoopes and S. Sharpless Townsend in 1849 in Wilmington, Delaware. In 1852 the firm was moved to Broad and Buttonwood Streets in Philadelphia. When Barton Hoopes died, his three sons took over: Barton Jr., Clement R. and Dawson. The area occupied by the company became known as Hoopeston. Almost all press received by the company was favorable until Election Day of 1906 when Dawson Hoopes tracked

The only known photograph of the Hoopes and Townsend Steel Mill, which was located near what is presently the Pennsylvania Turnpike interchange in Fort Washington. *Courtesy of George Haggar.*

down Charles A. Newhall in Ambler and shot him. The *Ambler Gazette* carried little news of the incident when it occurred until the case was ready to come to trial. Hoopes's attorney argued in March of 1907 that his client was not stable enough to stand trial since he had been in Kirkbride's Insane Hospital since the shooting. The judge ordered a trial date for early June 1907. Hoopes failed to appear that day, but he did show up later in the week. Before the imposing of the sentence by Judge Swartz, the story of the crime was retold. "Sensational allegations were made as to the motives which impelled Hoopes to shoot Newhall." Apparently Mr. Newhall, Chestnut Hill resident and clubman, had been seeing Katie E. Hoopes, Dawson Hoopes's wife. The Newhalls and the Hoopes lived next door to each other on West Chestnut Hill Avenue in the Chestnut Hill section of the city. The possibility exists that an affair was going on between Mrs. Hoopes and Mr. Newhall, but based on the behavior of Dawson Hoopes, the allegations may have been true only in his mind. However, Newhall did not seem to protest the allegations. Hoopes pled guilty and was convicted of the crime, fined $1,000 and ordered to serve one year in the county jail. Both sides agreed that Hoopes was not responsible at the time of the shooting due to temporary insanity and drunkenness. That, coupled with Hoopes's plea that his being jailed would probably kill his aged mother, caused the judge to indefinitely suspend the sentence with the caveat that Hoopes must keep the peace, especially with Newhall. Hoopes also had to put up $6,000 in bail money, which was supplied by his brothers. The *Gazette* reported that "it would also be agreed that Hoopes should be sent out of the country at once, as arrangements had been made whereby the prisoner would go on a trip around the world, starting Tuesday."

More than two years later, an August 9, 1909 account in the *Ambler Gazette* detailed another Dawson Hoopes appearance in court. He was now suing his brothers, Barton and Clement, to recover his holdings in Hoopes and Townsend, which they had held for him while he was out of the country. He also wanted the court to cancel an agreement he had made to pay his wife $2,500 a year. He further brought suit for divorce from Katie Hoopes, naming Charles A. Newhall correspondent.

Little was heard of Hoopes or his wife after that court appearance. Neither appears in the 1910 or 1920 census. Mrs. Hoopes may have remarried and changed her name, making her difficult to track. Dawson Hoopes is listed in the 1930 census in Philadelphia living alone in a rental unit, divorced and working as an engineer for a tool and die company. Charles Newhall appears in the 1910 census in the same Wilson Eyre Jr. designed house in Chestnut Hill he had occupied since 1885. His wife Phoebe is also there as well as some of his children. However, in 1920 the seventy-three-year old Mr. Newhall is listed as a resident of Hudson, New York, with a second wife, Katherine Clark Hudson, two of her sisters and a brother. At first glance Newhall seems to have married the ex-Mrs. Hoopes, but the discrepancy in age and birthplace indicates that this woman is a different person. Separate documents about the genealogy of his family show that the Clarks and Newhalls were related by marriage and that this woman was the cousin of Joseph Sill Clark, who later became mayor of Philadelphia.

ALONG THE PIKE

THE WHITEMARSH TRIANGLE

As early as 1698, records indicate the existence of Old Bethlehem Road. The highway had numerous names over the years and is known today as Bethlehem Pike. Businesses and houses began to appear along the highway as the area developed. Bethlehem Pike stretched from Philadelphia to Bethlehem and Easton. The section of the highway located in what was Fort Washington extends from its intersection with the Skippack Pike to just below Highland Avenue.

The lower end of Bethlehem Pike in Fort Washington is home to St. Thomas's Episcopal Church. Between 1690 and 1700 Edward Farmar donated land on which the church was built. The original log cabin structure burned in 1710 and was replaced with a second edifice that stood until it was replaced in 1858. Much more extensive history has been written about the church, and a short excerpt can be found in *Montgomery County: The Second Hundred Years*. The 1858 structure stands today and was the spiritual home of the most influential and moneyed families of Fort Washington. The *Ambler Gazette* covered numerous weddings at the church attended by Philadelphia society. Fort Washingtonians buried in the cemetery include members of the Bodenstein, Van Rensselaer, Fell, Pardee, Craig, Richmond, Nash and Goodrich families.

Adjacent to St. Thomas's sits a triangle of land formed by the convergence of Bethlehem Pike, Skippack Pike and Mather Lane. This site was home to some of the earliest development on this portion of the road. The oldest records indicate that several small structures were erected on this location in addition to a mill and tannery. One of those structures served as a tavern known as the Blue House. Its location appears to have been along Bethlehem Pike before 1782, where 574 Bethlehem Pike stands today. The land and buildings went through numerous owners and were purchased in 1901 by Rondo W. Zeitz, who constructed a new hotel on the site and called it the Fort Side Inn. In 1905, Zeitz sold the property to William P. Green, who made significant improvements to the structure and

Fort Side Inn matchbook cover.

its décor. Green's structural changes in the Colonial Revival style predominate the building to this day. Reports of the changes indicated that in 1910, Green hired the architects Sauer and Hahn of Philadelphia to reinvent the Fort Side Inn. The work was done by David McCrork. By June of 1911 the *Ambler Gazette* announced that the dining room would have a Japanese décor and a new sideboard from J.B. Van Sciver. In 1916, 475 yards of carpeting from Strawbridge and Clothier would be installed. Every week the *Gazette* carried reports of activities taking place at the Fort Side. Shooting competitions were a regular activity as were auctions of livestock. The January 13, 1898 *Gazette* mentioned that Charles Aiman, horse dealer and cattle drover, had established permanent headquarters at the inn and would have horses and cows always on hand. One local historian, Heinze Heineman, has written the most complete account about the Fort Side Inn, and a copy of his work is available at the Historical Society of Fort Washington.

Near the inn a mill was built along the Wissahickon Creek by Edward Farmar, son of Major Jasper Farmar, about 1686. It burned and was rebuilt by a later owner, Joseph Mather. Its last private owner was Calvin Pardee of nearby Church Hill Hall. He converted the mill into an indoor tennis court and used part for furniture storage. At the current time the mill is owned and operated in conjunction with Hope Lodge by the State of Pennsylvania and the Friends of Farmar Mill.

Mather built himself a fine house near the mill but fronting on the road at 560 Bethlehem Pike. The *Gazette* published a few different dates for the house including 1783 and 1815. Frank Godey, son of the publisher of *Godey's Lady's Book*, purchased this house in 1896 and lived there until he sold it to Calvin Pardee in 1912. Mr. Godey made significant improvements to the house, including the addition of electricity, although he retained an old windmill on the property. In a rare interview with the *Ambler Gazette*, Mr. Godey disclosed that his "only and constant companion [was] his secretary, Charles Magill." There was no female help employed on the premises. Once in a great while Mr. Godey hosted a small dinner for a few personal friends—all men. In his book *Calvin Pardee*, William G. Foulke recorded his grandfather's recollection of Mr. Godey, who annually gave "a hilarious neighborhood party on New Year's Eve" but was a "confirmed woman-hater." He also shared the fact that Mr. Godey's secretary, Mr. Magill, was "a dwarf commonly known as 'the squire.'"

Just north of the Godey house at 552 Bethlehem Pike is a house built by Joseph Mather for his daughter between 1830 and 1835. Prior to 1905, Calvin Pardee purchased this property to give to his daughter Helen as a wedding gift. Helen was married to Walter Longfellow Foulke, son of a prominent Montgomery County lawyer. The Foulkes lived here until they sold the house in 1914 to Cushman Newhall.

The most impressive structure in this section of Fort Washington is Hope Lodge. This fine example of Georgian architecture was built by Samuel Morris in the 1740s. After his death in 1770, the property passed to his brother Joshua. Its last private owners, William and Alice Degn rescued the house from the Keasbey and Mattison Company, who planned to tear it down and extend the nearby limestone quarry. The Degns willed the house and grounds to the Hope Lodge Foundation and today the property is administered by the Pennsylvania Historical and Museum Commission and the Friends of Hope Lodge.

Cover of *Godey's Ladies Book*.

Additional structures existed on this portion of Bethlehem Pike but appear to be of little significance in the history of the area. Some are of modest design and may well have been built as rental properties. E.H. Potts owned a number of these smaller houses near the present day Pennsylvania Turnpike overpass. Although some of these houses (528, 530 and 532 Bethlehem Pike) appear to be pre-Revolutionary, determining whether they are included on maps before the twentieth century is difficult since so many different buildings existed on Potts's property. The federal census of 1880 shows that Potts was a carpenter, so he may have built the structures himself or he may have purchased land with existing buildings. Since so many laborers on farms and estates in the area needed housing, these may have been tenant houses.

ABOVE HOPE LODGE

When Samuel Morris of Hope Lodge died in 1770, he stipulated that a Protestant free school be established to serve children within a mile and a half radius. The Union School was built in 1773 and served the community until 1869, when it became overcrowded. The building became known as Lyceum Hall and was the site of lectures, concerts and public meetings. The building is currently used as both a commercial and residential facility. In 1869 Whitemarsh Township built the Whitemarsh Public School to relieve the overcrowding of the Union School. By 1918 the new school was overcrowded and some classes were moved to the Union School. Today this structure houses a privately run daycare center called the Hey Diddle Diddle Day School.

An early twentieth-century photograph of Hope Lodge prior to restoration.

The Whitemarsh School on Bethlehem Pike.

Another result of the will of Samuel Morris was the sale of a small parcel of land for five shillings to the Society of Friends in 1791 for the purpose of erecting a place of worship for their monthly meetings. The Friends included Joseph Mather, Joseph Cleaver and Joseph Lukens. Maps indicate the Friends owned the land until almost 1926. The Meeting House at Plymouth is often the only one referred to in Whitemarsh Township. A building does exist at this location today (515 Bethlehem Pike), but whether this is the original structure is impossible to determine.

Lying just north of the schools at 508 Bethlehem Pike was the summer estate of Pierre Camblos, born to a Philadelphia banker and his wife. By 1860 Pierre's father's fortune topped $100,000. In 1885 Camblos married Ellen Lyle Morris, who was descended from some of the earliest Philadelphians and was a relative of Samuel Morris of Hope Lodge. Camblos was a true gentleman farmer, and each summer for a number of years he was harvesting fruit on his property at the beginning of June. He also produced hogs close to four hundred pounds. Together Pierre and Ellen Camblos had four children, but Ellen died in 1900 at the age of forty-one. Camblos remained at the farm for at least part of the next ten years, during which he played Santa to his neighbors at Christmas, giving candy to the kids and turkeys to the adults. In September of 1909, Camblos sold his farm to Daniel Buckley, who had been summering in Newport. Three months later the

Gazette mentioned that Buckley's birds had defeated those of William Frazier Harrison of Ridgewood Farm at an annual contest. Buckley appears on the property the following year in the 1910 census with his wife, one son and five servants. Pierre Camblos was noted in the 1910 census as having remarried and relocated to Washington, D.C., close to where his son was playing football for the University of Virginia.

Sections of Fort Washington State Park were created from land belonging to Mrs. A.H. Bolton on one side of Bethlehem Pike and Mrs. E.S. Richards on the other. Both women were the daughters of Jacob Haines, once proprietor of the Fort Side Inn. Mrs. Richards's property, Old Fort Farm, was used by the family but in later years became a rental property. At the back of her fifteen acre tract was the Redoubt, where Washington and his men repulsed the attack of the British who were marching up from Germantown in 1777. In 1897 the Union Traction Company offered the Richards $20,000 for their land. The plan was to build an amusement park there. The offer was rejected, and the company purchased land along Bethlehem Pike closer to Chestnut Hill later that year and built Chestnut Hill Park. Mrs. Richards kindly allowed residents of Fort Washington to hold their annual Memorial Day ceremony on her land. Her house still stands at 509 Bethlehem Pike and is a private residence. The rest of her Old Fort Farm was sold to the Commonwealth of Pennsylvania by her daughter, Annie Richards, in April of 1929 for $24,000. After 1930 Mrs. Bolton's property became part of Fort Washington State Park and is now home to the park superintendent.

The stone house at 491 Bethlehem Pike, now Robinson's Flagstone, was built by George Washington Stout circa 1870. Stout bought the land prior in 1868, and since he was a stonemason, it's fair to assume he built the place himself. In 1880 he was residing there with his wife Sarah and three children, but in 1897, after the deaths of his wife and son Jacob, he and his housekeeper, Ellen Rittenhouse, moved to a new house in the Heights.

Bisecting Bethlehem Pike in the heart of Fort Washington is the Sandy Run Creek, which proved to be an impediment to travelers when it flooded. An inn was built near the creek called the Sandy Run Tavern, but its exact location is unknown. Accounts of Revolutionary War soldiers from the Whitemarsh Encampment frequenting the tavern are common but unsubstantiated. The local lore indicates that the tavern burned in 1791.

In 1801 Henry Daub built a new two-story stone establishment known as the Sandy Run Hotel on the banks of the Sandy Run Creek. The hotel changed hands many times, the transactions often involving the sheriff. An alleged 1857 fire resulted in the addition of the third floor and installation of a flat roofline. Sometime between 1859 and 1873 the name was changed to the Clifton House. Scholars differ on whether Daniel Blyler or William Witte instituted the change, but the new name reflected that the hotel sat on a cliff in close proximity to a nearby quarry. Blyler was the first proprietor of the inn to realize its potential as a destination for summer boarders from Philadelphia, since it was so close to the train station. The Historical Society of Fort Washington has several sources in its collections by Eleanor Ward Altemus and Edward T. Addison Jr., which give more details about the many owners of Clifton House.

In this rare photograph of Clifton House the annex that helped serve the summer clients is visible. The Clifton House was an upscale summer resort into the first decades of the twentieth century. *Courtesy of Nick Jennings.*

The popularity of the hotel reached its zenith during the ownership of George Herman, whose wife's parents owned nearby Hope Lodge. To attract summer visitors, Herman added numerous activities for the enjoyment of his guests. Vacationers could hike through the picturesque Whitemarsh Valley, fish or swim in the Sandy Run, ride horses, hire a carriage, or play croquet while enjoying the cool, fresh air of the country. Herman was also responsible for adding buildings to the property including an annex that was used for banquets and balls as well as musical and literary entertainment. Two notations carried by the *Ambler Gazette* in 1898 reveal Herman's business acumen. First the annual ball was held on August 3 for two hundred guests in the annex decorated with plants and flags and featuring Larry's Orchestra of Philadelphia. The other report stated that in preparation for the 1899 season, Herman extended his porch on the annex so that visitors could step directly onto the porch from their carriages. He would also provide refreshments for cyclists and other travelers passing by on Bethlehem Pike. Although Herman owned the property for many years, by the summer of 1903, the local paper reported that Miss Mary Lee would run the Clifton House for the season. She was just one of many proprietors of the inn during Herman's tenure.

The advent of the automobile signaled the end of the Clifton House as a desirable destination. Occasionally the *Gazette* would report on a large event at Clifton House, like a wedding for four hundred people in October of 1919. For the most part, however, Clifton House continued to decline until the structure was abandoned and in disrepair. Herman sold the property, buildings, stone quarry and thirty acres in 1919 to Samuel Nemorofsky for $15,500, and for the next eleven years it went rapidly through the hands of three different owners before becoming the property of the Fairmount Park Commission. Their plan was to extend the Wissahickon Drive along the Sandy Run Creek to Fort Washington State Park. When this plan fell through, the future of Clifton House was uncertain. The annex was torn down in 1932.

At about the same time, a group of local citizens organized an historical society for the purpose of studying the history and folklore of Montgomery County and especially the Whitemarsh area. In 1935 they organized the Historical Society of Fort Washington. Its first officers were Mrs. J. Howard Buck, president; Mrs. W. George Bardens, vice-president; Mrs. Russell Conover, treasurer; Mrs. Mark Z. McGill, recording secretary; Mrs. Robert James Keppel, corresponding secretary; Mrs. T. Duncan Just, headquarters chairman; and Mrs. Allan M. Craig, parliamentarian. Membership grew to one hundred members in the first year. Concerned about the loss of Clifton House, the group worked with former Governor Gifford Pinchot of Pennsylvania to save the structure. With his assistance, the Works Progress Administration (WPA) restored the building. After the work was completed, the newly renovated building was leased to the society for one dollar a year beginning in 1937. The society continues to maintain the building and keep it open to the public. Not only is it the base of operations for its efforts with regard to local history but it is also the venue for monthly programs open to the public. In addition to museum rooms, the building houses a fine research library dedicated to local history. Over the years members have volunteered time, materials and historic artifacts to enhance this community resource.

Mrs. J. Howard Buck, first president of the Historical Society of Fort Washington. *Courtesy of Robert and Gladys Buck.*

In addition to the historical society, the American Legion Post was a vital part of Fort Washington life. Many young men from Fort Washington served their country during World War I, and a plaque at the rear of the Trinity Lutheran Church commemorates their service. The plaque reads:

Honor Roll
World War 1917–1919

World War #1 Veterans
This Tablet is erected in Honor of the men of Fort Washington PA who served in the Victorious War for Democracy

Anshutz, Edward R.
Besore, C.J.
Bimson, Arthur
Bossard, Harvey
Brinker, Warren
Bytheway, Phillip
Cadwalader, Charles
Cadwalader, Gouverneur
Cadwalader, Thomas
Craig, A.J., MD
Craig, Allan M. Jr.
Fehrer, Charles A.
Foulke, Walter L.
Funk, Harold S.
Gordon, Robert, 3rd
Henry, Howard H.
Hippeli, Otto
Hobensack, Chester
Huffnagle, George
James, Melvin
Jordan, Isaac
Kittson, James Gordon
Klosterman, Luther C.
Klosterman, Warren W.
Leaf, Charles Leonard
McAdoo, Henry M.
Michener, Ralph
Morris, Charles
Morris, John

Murphy, Edward
Murphy, Harry
Murray, David
Neurath, Earnest
Oberholtzer, Henry
Ralston, Kenneth
Sigmund, Ralph
Spohn, Francis
Stearly, Irving H.
Tease, Cameron
Tidmarsh, Henry
Van Lear, William
Wallace, Romine
Walt, Joseph
Weber, Frank Jr.
Weikert, Earl D.
Wilson, James M. Jr.
Winterbottom, Joseph
Woodbury, Charles Crawford
Yarnall, Robert M. Jr.
Yeakle, William R.

Following World War I, a group of veterans met at the rectory of St. Thomas Church at the invitation of Reverend N.B. Groton. They applied to the state headquarters for a temporary chapter under the name of Whitemarsh Post and were given the designation of American Legion Post, No. 10. They later decided to adopt the name William Boulton Dixon Post, No. 10 to honor a local hero of World War I. William Boulton Dixon was born in Philadelphia and later graduated from Princeton University in 1915. He enlisted at the outbreak of the war and was commissioned a first lieutenant. Dixon was killed by a direct hit of a German field gun near Thiaucourt, France, on October 17, 1918. He was the first young man from this area to die in the war. No connection has been found between Dixon and the Boltons who owned land near the post. Dixon's father was a wealthy Philadelphia banker. His brother, Fitz Eugene Dixon, married Eleanor Widener. Eleanor's brother, George D. Widener, owned Erdenheim Farms, located nearby in Whitemarsh. Widener was one of the first officers for the post. The first elected officers were Dr. E.B. Krumbhaar, commander; C.N. Wolfe, vice-commander; L.C. Klosterman, adjutant; George D. Widener, finance officer; Earl D. Weikert, historian; and Reverend N.B. Groton, honorary chaplain. In the early days the post held meetings at a house owned by Mrs. Emily Vaux that was next to the Whitemarsh post office on Bethlehem Pike near Mather Lane. Beginning in 1930 the post purchased and moved its base of operations to the Conard Auger Mill located directly across Bethlehem Pike from Clifton House.

Memorial Day parade on Bethlehem Pike. *Courtesy of William Boulton Dixon, Post #10.*

The post was very active in Memorial Day activities at Fort Hill. These events predated the legion and were initiated by two other organizations. The Junior Order of United American Mechanics (JOUAM) placed the first flagpole at Fort Hill on July 4, 1887. They were based at Wissahickon Hall, which they built in 1888 at what is now 451 Bethlehem Pike. In 1900, the JOUAM had the first flag raising on the hill on Memorial Day. Addresses were made by Senator John A. Wentz and others. The need for an organization to hold yearly observations on Memorial Day was recognized, and the Fort Hill Memorial Association was formed. Its first president was George Bodenstein, who was succeeded by Samuel Yeakle, and in the 1930s officers included David McCrork, president; Luther C. Klosterman, secretary; and U.G. Funk, treasurer. From its inception, the legion post participated in the Memorial Day commemoration and once they moved to the Auger Mill site, they assumed a leading role in the day. One annual element of the commemoration from the start was a parade down Bethlehem Pike to Fort Hill. In addition to these organizations marchers included the 103rd Engineer Band, fire companies, three Fort Washington lodges, two Flourtown lodges, Boy Scouts, Girl Scouts, public school children from three townships, fire companies, bands and service organizations. Memorial services took place at Trinity Lutheran Church on Summit Avenue followed by floral tributes by elementary students at three cemeteries. Military exhibitions, drum and bugle corps presentations, harmonica band presentations, baseball games and lunches filled the afternoon hours. In later years the day ended with dinner and dancing. In the late 1930s the Veterans Home Association of Whitemarsh purchased a building and property that abuts Fort Hill. This site serves as the present-day home of the William Boulton Dixon Post, No. 10. The structure was built by William and Amanda Garner in 1881.

The old Auger Mill became the home of the American Legion Post in 1930. Pictured are the first officers of the post. *Courtesy of the Historical Society of Fort Washington.*

THE VILLAGE CENTER

Near the intersection of the railroad and Bethlehem Pike, businesses flourished. There merchants established drug stores, a bakery, a general store, a barber shop, a meat store, a wagon repair shop, a livery stable, an oyster bay and a lumber and coal yard. Some of the merchants who provided services and products were residents of the Heights while others lived along Bethlehem Pike. In 1918 William Oberholtzer, who had been operating the store in Masonic Hall, now Rich's Deli, after Fred Huffnagle, sold to G.E. Ritter of West Philadelphia. In 1910 the *Gazette* released details about J.M. Brock, who operated Marsden Kennels in Fort Washington. Known for Airedales, Brock took prizes at dog shows in Boston, Coney Island and New York City. James Craig's pharmacy on Summit Avenue near the train station was a local gathering place for residents. Craig had the first phone line in the area, and news of the store and Craig's family was included weekly in the *Gazette*. His son, Albert J. Craig, grew up to be the doctor who delivered most babies in the Heights for decades. His office was located in part of his father's drugstore. He was appointed assistant surgeon of gynecology at St. Luke's Hospital in Philadelphia. James Craig had other sons: Walter graduated from Temple University in the pharmacy program in 1913, and Thomas, whose health was frail, died in 1909 at the age of twenty-eight. Another son, William, who worked for Midvale Steel Company, also died at the age of twenty-eight. James Craig himself died in 1919 and is buried at St. Thomas's. He had been in the drugstore business in Fort Washington for twenty-two years after starting his career on Butler Avenue in Ambler.

Helen Bodenstein and beau enjoy a summer day at Dungan's. *Courtesy of Beatrice Bodenstein.*

One of the largest properties in the village center belonged to the Conard (Conrad) family. Albert Conard purchased an existing gristmill on Sandy Run Creek in the mid-nineteenth century and began making augers or drill bits with his brother Isaac. In addition to the mill, the property had an existing house, which was built for Henry Daub about 1805, at what is now 488 Bethlehem Pike. Daub built the Sandy Run Hotel in 1801 and was also operator of the mill at one time. During the Conards' tenure at the mill, Albert's son, John Conard, purchased part of the property and built a house for himself at what is now 478 Bethlehem Pike in 1879. John Conard also conducted the federal census locally in 1900 and 1910 and in 1907 had a column in the *Gazette* with information about the Whitemarsh Encampment reprinted from an earlier paper, the *Sentinel.* Albert Conard's daughter married B. Wallace Mammel, and records indicate they also lived on the property. Mammel had a small farm and home market and later added a milk route. The Conard family sold the mill and property in 1905 to the newly formed Wissahickon Electric Company. In 1912 part of the mill property became the Fort Washington Auto and Machine Shop. 478 Bethlehem Pike was sold to a Mr. Corcoran, and 488 Bethlehem Pike and the acreage behind was sold to John Kulp.

The Honorable John Adam Wentz, state senator. *Courtesy of Ellwood Roberts.*

The village center was also home to the largest athletic field and swimming hole in Fort Washington, known as Dungan's Field. Elmer Dungan was a successful businessman in furniture, jewelry and clocks. He was such a community-minded person that when he purchased his property in Fort Washington in 1904, he allowed anyone who wanted to use his property for recreation to do so free of charge as long as they followed the rules. In 1912 Dungan purchased the portion of the Conard Mill property on the north side of Sandy Run Creek. His land then included a baseball diamond, swimming lake, tennis courts and a bowling green. His two sons, Allen and Warren, were both members of a semi-professional baseball team. In March of 1920, Elmer Dungan had a clock, three feet in diameter, mounted on his house so that sportsmen and women knew when it was time to go home. The clock can still be seen on the side of Zake's Cakes, located at 444 Bethlehem Pike.

Many notable people lived on or near Bethlehem Pike. One of the most prestigious residents was the honorable John Adam Wentz, who lived at 7177 Lafayette Avenue. He was born in Whitemarsh on November 1, 1858. Ellwood Roberts, author of *The Biographical Annals of Montgomery County*, was his instructor at the Whitemarsh School and later included Wentz's biography in his book. At the age of seventeen, John Adam Wentz decided not to continue in the family business of farming and instead went to Philadelphia as a plumber's apprentice. He soon assumed positions as a bookkeeper and salesman. By 1904, John Wentz was a representative of Fleck Brothers, the largest plumbing supply house in Philadelphia. During this time, his involvement in local affairs increased. He served three times as the auditor of Springfield Township. In 1891 he served as jury commissioner and was elected to the Ambler School Board in 1894. His election to the board spoke of his outstanding character. He was able to win election despite the fact that his ward had four registered Republicans to one Democrat, and John Wentz was a Democrat. Further evidence of the respect accorded him was the fact that the board, of which he was the only Democrat, unanimously selected him as board president. He later served as chairman of the State School Directors Association. Wentz's involvement in the community extended beyond the school board. He was an active member of the Fort Washington Lodge 308 of the Free and Accepted Masons and Lodge 1123 of the International Order of Odd Fellows. Elected to the State Senate in 1898, John Wentz served the Commonwealth admirably. Appointed to numerous committees, he authored many pieces of legislation during his term. His efforts transcended party lines and were viewed as moral and highly principled for that time. An advocate for improving public education in the state and honest government, John Wentz was praised by many.

The Wentz name is found on other properties in the area as well, as in nearby Worcester, Pennsylvania. John Wentz's great-grandfather was one of three brothers who came from Germany in the mid-eighteenth century and settled in Worcester Township. Besides owning a large tract of land, the brothers built the Wentz Reformed Church. The families were prosperous and populated the Worcester area. John Wentz's grandfather, Jonathan Wentz, married Elizabeth Sheetz of Whitemarsh, settled here and became a prominent citizen.

Hattie Theel, historian and lifelong resident of Fort Washington. *Courtesy of the Historical Society of Fort Washington.*

Jonathan Wentz was a farmer, miller and lime burner. George Hocker Wentz, John Wentz's father, married Sarah A. Wentz when he was nineteen years old. She was the daughter of a distant relative, Jacob Wentz, who helped organize the Union Church on Bethlehem Pike, now known as Zion Lutheran Church. Jacob Wentz owned and resided at Hope Lodge until his death in 1855 when the property went to his son Thomas.

Any history of Fort Washington must include Henrietta Oberholtzer Theel. Known to all as Hattie, she was born on March 18, 1899, and lived at 441 Bethlehem Pike. Her father, Henry Oberholtzer, was listed in the census as a house painter but was mentioned numerous times in the *Gazette* as a painter of carriages. Besides Hattie, the other Oberholtzer children included John and Henry. Hattie attended the Union School where she became keenly interested in history. She continued her studies at Drexel University and graduated in 1918. Hattie married Percival Theel on August 12, 1920, and the couple moved to Jarrettown. Following a fire at their house, they returned to the house on Bethlehem Pike. For many people, Hattie was the historian of Fort Washington. She served in that capacity for numerous organizations including the Historical Society of Fort Washington, The Ladies Auxiliary of the Fort Hill Memorial Association and the Questers. Many members of the historical society recall that Hattie would offer a story of local history at the start of each meeting. In 1976, she was a nominee for the Gimbel Award for Woman of the Year. The death of this colorful historian on December 7, 1991, was a tremendous loss for Fort Washington.

Documents indicate that Wonderly's Inn sat on the west side of Bethlehem Pike north of Sandy Run Creek. In 1855 with the arrival of the railroad in Fort Washington, a new hotel was built to accommodate the needs of train travelers. The Fort Washington Hotel, also known as the Fort Washington House, was built on the site of the former inn. Guests of the hotel were among those who aided the victims of the horrific train wreck of 1856 in nearby Camp Hill. This was the first hotel or inn along Bethlehem Pike that did not have its origin in the stagecoach traffic. This hotel represents the influence that the train had on the area as an impetus for growth and development. Carpenter Gothic in design, the hotel served as home to the local Masonic Lodge from 1857 until 1868. The proprietor of the hotel in 1897 was Mr. Erb. By 1901 Robert Gordon Jr. placed a new sign at the hotel indicating his involvement with the establishment. Soon after that, a report appeared that he was extending the dining room and adding a bay window. In August of 1903, a reporter for the *Gazette* wrote, "Mr. Gordon has greatly beautified and improved the interior of the famous old stand." The article described the walls as decorated with heads of elk and antelope. Depiction of other wildlife included ducks, flying ducks, birds and fish. Local resident George Maust was in charge of the stables and yard at the hotel in 1904.

A row of modest dwellings run from the railroad toward Wissahickon Hall. These structures are of a variety of mid-nineteenth century architectural style. Phillip Fisher owned four of the buildings, which the *Gazette* called his tenant houses. John Matlack and Van Winkle owned properties here too. The village blacksmith, John Gillian, operated his business here for twenty-five years.

Wissahickon Hall, located on Bethlehem Pike, provided a meeting location for the young community. *Courtesy of the Historical Society of Fort Washington.*

Just across the train tracks was a house belonging to Abram Carn and his family. The structure served as an early post office and general store for Fort Washington. After the death of Abram Carn in 1904, the store was taken over by Ambler druggist Rees Roberts, who opened Ye Olde Fort Drug Store. The Carn family remained active in Fort Washington affairs for many years. The building had other uses and owners throughout the twentieth century, but the structure was torn down in 2003 to expand parking for a local car dealer.

In 1881 David Knipe bought land from William Shaffer to start a business. He ran a very successful lumberyard and coal yard in what is now the Septa parking lot. He erected a building that soon contained other businesses including a plumbing establishment, a barbershop and a bakery. In 1903 Knipe sued the North Pennsylvania Railroad for loss of ground when they expanded their operations. About three months later, in 1904, he sold

Thomas P. Anshutz, cofounder of the Darby School of Art and head instructor of the Pennsylvania Academy of Fine Arts in Philadelphia. *Courtesy of the Philadelphia Sketch Club.*

his ground and business to Samuel Yeakle of Whitemarsh, the son of Senator William A. Yeakle. Knipe lived in Ambler but owned other ground along Bethlehem Pike stretching back to the railroad near Morris Road. In 1920 the *Gazette* ran a story, "The Fort to Boom?" which detailed the erection of eighty houses on land belonging to Knipe and the Flues family. A developer had the idea of locating a Hebrew village on the site. Apparently the idea never materialized, and in 1926, Knipe sold his land to John M. Kennedy Jr., who planned to have W.D. Neal build him a modest twenty houses.

The building opposite the Carn property is wonderful example of Italianate architecture. The 1871 and 1891 maps of Fort Washington indicate that the property was owned by William Shaffer. Shaffer made purchases in Whitemarsh in 1865 and 1869, but dating the property through tax records is difficult because Shaffer owned so much land in the area. Since this architectural style was popular around the middle of the century, Shaffer probably built the house by 1870 or bought the property with an already existing structure. The building has been home to a number of different owners and businesses in the twentieth century and still stands in excellent condition at 416 Bethlehem Pike.

ABOVE PENNSYLVANIA AVENUE

The popular Toner's Old Beef and Ale appears to be an eighteenth century establishment but was actually built in 1925 by the Potts Brothers. The building was originally a brick

The Anshutz home at 212 Bethlehem Pike. *Courtesy of Marybeth Barba.*

store and dwelling. The truly old structure on this section of the old turnpike stands at 215 Bethlehem Pike. The Window Pane Tax of 1798 indicates one house on the east side of Bethlehem Pike north of Pennsylvania Avenue. Casper Schlater Jr. built this house in 1795, which stood apart from other structures. By 1850 a few farmhouses were located close by, but this area did not develop into a neighborhood until much later.

Across Bethlehem Pike from the Schlater house are some buildings that were once part of an early twentieth century art school. Thomas Anshutz was a student at the Pennsylvania Academy of the Fine Arts (PAFA), studying principally under Thomas Eakins from 1876–1880. Upon his graduation he was asked to join the faculty. In 1898 he founded the Darby School of Painting, along Darby Creek in West Chester, with his former student and fellow instructor at PAFA, Hugh Breckenridge. In 1899 after buying an old house at 212 Bethlehem Pike in Fort Washington, Anshutz decided to move the school there. The property had belonged to William E. Towne and included a stable and almost five acres of ground. By spring of 1901 Breckenridge had a house, which he called Phloxdale, built at 208 Bethlehem Pike. The third floor studio had an enormous window to let in a lot of natural light. The men also used the Orchards at 222 Bethlehem Pike to house some of their students. Several studio buildings were added to the grounds of the school and provided studio space for students, although much of the painting was done outdoors.

Hugh Breckenridge, cofounder of the Darby School of Art and owner of 208 Bethlehem Pike. *Courtesy of Philadelphia Sketch Club.*

The school was popular with both men and women, and although not an official extension of PAFA, many of the students from the academy spent their summers studying with Anshutz and Breckenridge, including Daniel Garber and H. Lyman Sayen. When they returned to PAFA in the fall, the students had an exhibit of the work they produced during the summer. A now defunct Philadelphia newspaper, the *North American*, did an extensive spread on the Darby School on Sunday, July 25, 1909, which can be summed up in these words of the reporter:

Life at the Darby School is a next-to-nature affair, lived for art's sake alone…[The students] *break up into groups if the group cannot agree upon the same rural scene for an inspiration. One day last week the whole class set up their camp stools in the middle of the Wissahickon Creek…In his own studio, which is sought by the leading artists of the country, Mr. Anshutz, the chief inspiration of the school, spoke of the aims and motive. He believes that more can be accomplished in three months' summer school work than in nine in a city art school, and declares that the incentive of nature and the inspiration caught from studying "the meaning and the music" of life in the open air is worth a scholarship to a student.*

The students were also treated to some social evenings organized by Breckenridge. The *Ambler Gazette* ran stories each season about some of these. In July of 1901, Mr. Breckenridge had an outdoor gathering for the students featuring Chinese and Japanese lanterns and a Chinese dance. That same summer he took the young painters on a straw ride to nearby Willow Grove Park.

The Darby School ran from the beginning of June until the end of September each summer until 1910. Enrollment in the classes was steady through the ten years the school operated, but Breckenridge and Anshutz grew apart, and Anshutz's health began to fail. The last two seasons Anshutz ran the school by himself while Breckenridge was pursuing his own career.

The Darby School and the presence of Anshutz in Fort Washington attracted other artists from PAFA to visit Fort Washington. Alexander Calder is known to have

John Sloan, American artist. *Courtesy of Philadelphia Sketch Club.*

summered here. Another well-known visitor was John Sloan, one of "The Eight" who are credited with starting the Ashcan School of Painting. Sloan had studied with Anshutz at PAFA. At first he worked as an illustrator for newspapers and magazines in Philadelphia, but after his marriage, he moved to New York City. He continued to visit Fort Washington regularly since his parents and two sisters had moved to 210 Madison Avenue from Lock Haven, Pennsylvania. His sister, Marianna Sloan, was also an artist specializing in watercolors, who sometimes found work illustrating books. Sloan kept a diary from 1906–13, and a number of the entries detailed his visits to the family in Fort Washington. He often brought along his good friend and fellow artist, Samuel Butler Yeats, father of the Irish poet. Sloan's diaries were reproduced in a 1965 book, *John Sloan's New York Scene.*

Two twentieth century developments grew at the northern edge of Fort Washington. The first was Ambler Highlands on the site of Reuben Berkenstock's farm. Land was purchased as building lots in 1907 by Dager and Knight. By 1916, more than a dozen houses had been built. The development was bordered by Bethlehem Pike, Highland Avenue and Dr. Elliger's estate. Dr. George Elliger purchased land and a house from Israim Engleman in 1855 and added acreage two years later. The Elliger estate was later sold to the Potts brothers and became known as Elliger Park. The Potts Brothers started to build here in the mid 1920s. Elliger Park and Ambler Highlands make up a lovely residential neighborhood containing a variety of housing styles nestled among mature shade trees.

While the majority of this book focuses on an earlier time period, an event that occurred in 1944 in Ambler Highlands had not only local significance but also national and international importance. One day at work Mrs. W. George (Bess) Bardens had an antique object on her desk. Many of the women in the office inquired about the object. Bardens, realizing that there was an interest in and a lack of knowledge of antiques, had an idea. On April 6, 1944, fourteen women were invited to Bardens's house at 512 Hartranft Avenue, just off Bethlehem Pike. Each woman was asked to bring a sandwich and an antique. Bardens had the idea of organizing a group to study and collect antiques. She wrote to Mr. Charles Stow, author of a *New York Sun* column called "The Quester" explaining her idea and asking permission to use the name "Questers". Mr. Stow approved and encouraged Mrs. Bardens in her efforts. The group, officially called the Countryside Questers grew to thirty-five women within its first year. A second club formed in the second year, and by the fifth year, Questers had six clubs including the Treasurers Questers, Wayside Questers, Town and Country Questers, Heirloom Questers and the Heritage Questers. The organization went national in 1950, and Mrs. Bardens served as its first president from 1950 to 1956. Other women from Fort Washington who served on the first national board were Mrs. Walt as second vice-president and Mrs. H. Chester Radcliffe as recording secretary. Committee chairs included Mrs. Percival Theel, who served as national historian from 1950 until 1963. From the start each club was independent but shared its work with other clubs through the national headquarters. They shared papers on antiques as well as potential speakers for meetings. Each April the national organization holds a luncheon featuring speakers on a variety of topics related to antiques. The Quester Organization encourages membership for people interested in collecting antiques and related subjects. While the early members were mostly women, men have joined the clubs in greater numbers in recent years. One of the main goals of the Quester Organization is to donate funds toward the restoration and preservation of historic sites. Many local historical institutions have benefited from the hard work and generosity of Quester groups.

3

LARGE ESTATES IN AND AROUND FORT WASHINGTON

While the Heights served the vacationer and the growing middle class, land around the Heights provided the setting for wealthy Philadelphians. Major estates were built just a short distance from the neighborhood.

CAMP HILL HALL, HAWKSWELL, EMLEN HOUSE

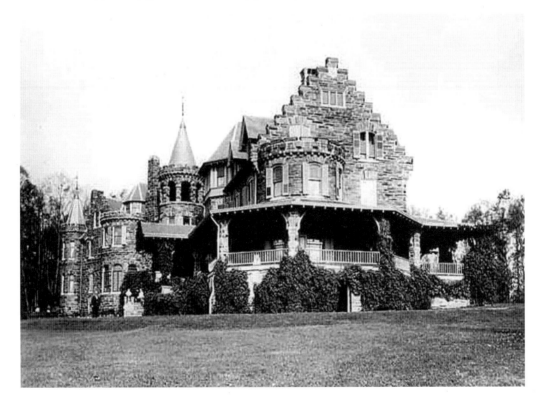

Camp Hill Hall. *Courtesy of Drexel Archives.*

John Ruckman Fell grew up in high society and in 1879, married Sarah Drexel, youngest daughter of A.J. Drexel of Philadelphia. John Fell followed his father, Joseph Gillingham Fell, in the firm of A. Pardee and Company, miners and shippers of coal. He was also a director of the Lehigh Valley Railroad, a member of the Philadelphia Park Commission and an executor and trustee under the will of the late A.J. Drexel. In 1882 John and Sarah Fell purchased land in the Whitemarsh Valley adjacent to the land owned by his father. They built a mansion on the top of the hill, leaving as much woodland as possible. While no architect is credited with designing the mansion, architects of record for later additions worked for T.P. Chandler early in their careers, indicating he could be the architect of the original structure. The estate, "Camp Hill," served as the country house of the couple when they were not at home at 313 South Broad Street. The Fells had four children: twin girls Amanda (Minnie) and Ellen, born 1880; Mae, born 1884; Frances, born 1887; and John, born 1889. Two tragedies struck the young family. In 1889 Ellen died, and on November 15, 1895, John R. Fell died of a stroke at the age of thirty-seven.

The death of her husband and father two years before did not place any financial burden on Sarah Drexel Fell. Her marriage to John Fell had merged two rich and respected families from Philadelphia society, and she was worth at least $10 million. Her late father was the dominant force in the Drexel banking empire. In 1897 Sarah built a lavish house at 1801 Walnut Street in Philadelphia. Designed by Peabody and Sterns of Boston at a

John R. Fell and Sarah Drexel Fell. *Courtesy of Grace Earwaker.*

Alexander Van Rensselaer, second husband of Sarah Drexel Fell. *Courtesy of Drexel Archives.*

cost of $250,000, the townhouse served as the family's city residence. After a sailing trip on her yacht *May* in August of 1897 with the Biddles and Alexander Van Rensselaer, Sarah Fell and Van Rensselaer announced that they were engaged. They were married less than six months later at Camp Hill Hall in Fort Washington on January 27, 1898.

Mr. Van Rensselaer, like his wife, came from great wealth. His ancestor, Kilian Van Rensselaer helped to found the Dutch East India Company. Although Kilian Van Rensselaer never came to America, he did send a younger family member to purchase a large tract of land near Albany, New York, from the local Native Americans. In 1851 Stephen Van Rensselaer, Alexander's grandfather, founded Rensselaer Polytechnic Institute, just about the time that Alexander Van Rensselaer was born to a clergyman and his wife in Burlington, New Jersey. Van Rensselaer excelled in his studies and attended Princeton, where he was captain of the football team in 1870.

During the summer of 1898, America was embroiled in the Spanish-American War, and many wealthy Americans volunteered the use of their yachts to the military. The Van Rensselaers placed the *May* at the disposal of the National Relief Commission. In August, after a few days of stripping at its owners' expense, the 228-foot yacht, carrying the commissioners, the Van Rensselaers, eighty tons of supplies and a corps of nurses, left the Arch Street pier bound for Puerto Rico. Alexander Van Rensselaer served as the first commodore of the Philadelphia chapter of the Corinthian Yacht Club, located on the Delaware River near Essington. He and his wife were avid sailors. They sold the *May* in 1911 for $100,000 and in 1913 let out contacts for a new yacht costing about $250,000.

Fell children aboard the *May* with staff and crew circa 1900. *Courtesy of John R. Fell, III.*

The Van Rensselaers also traveled by commercial means. Over the years they lived at Camp Hill Hall, the *Gazette* carried stories about their trips to Japan, China, India, the Suez Canal, Italy and France. During an eight-month excursion they were entertained by the Rajah of Singapore, the royal family of Japan and the Viceroy of India. Their most prestigious honor occurred when they were presented at the court of King James in 1911, presumably for the new British monarch, George V.

Over the course of their marriage, the Van Rensselaers made many improvements to the estate that were described in the local paper. In 1905 David McCrork built a squash court for Mrs. Van Rensselaer and an "automobile house." In 1907 Alexander Van Rensselaer added terraced garden areas with one hundred trees and shrubs and widened and bricked the driveway. In 1911 the architectural firm of Cope and Stewardson added a 30-foot by 62-foot wing to the mansion and made changes to the second and third floors at a cost of $30,000. On the west side of the building outside this new room is the Van Rensselaer crest. Local nurseryman Meehan constructed Italian gardens in 1915.

The Van Rensselaers were very kind and giving people. Every summer they brought several groups of underprivileged children out to Camp Hill for a two-week stay, and local children would come to the mansion at Christmas. The December 27, 1900 edition of the *Ambler Gazette* indicated that the Van Rensselaers, "known for their hospitality and Christian work in helping both the old and young, gave a Christmas dinner to about forty

Hawkswell. *Courtesy of Historical Society of Fort Washington.*

children of this place and the immediate vicinity of their Camp Hill residence on Tuesday (Christmas). Each girl was presented with a doll and every boy with a sled or express wagon and a box of candy." Any guest of the Van Rensselaers was made to feel important no matter what his personal wealth. Both were very interested in the Philadelphia Orchestra, and Mr. Van Rensselaer was its president from 1901 until 1933 when ill health and old age prevented him from continuing. During the 1918 coal shortage Sarah Van Rensselaer and daughter Mae Henry shared their coal with those in need.

All of Sarah Drexel Fell Van Rensselaer's children were very fond of their stepfather. On December 8, 1898, the couple held a lavish party to introduce Amanda (Minnie) Fell into society. A little over a year later she was married to Robert Kelso Cassatt, son of Alexander J. Cassatt, president of the Pennsylvania Railroad. The wedding was held at St. Thomas's Episcopal Church in Whitemarsh on January 22, 1900. The six hundred guests from the highest rung of society's ladder who traveled to the area by special train from the city completely filled the church. A reception followed at Camp Hill Hall.

On June 23, 1904, Mae, the second Fell daughter, married Howard Houston Henry. The couple subsequently resided just across the road from Camp Hill Hall at Hawkswell, which Mrs. Van Rensselaer had built for them by architect Wilson Eyre Jr. H.H. Henry served in World War I during which he died of a heart problem in 1918. A few years later on January 15, 1921, Mae married Gouverneur Cadwalader, whose brother Richard Cadwalader, lived next door at Fairwold.

Emlen House. *Courtesy of Historical Society of Fort Washington.*

Frances Paul Drexel Fell, the youngest of the three girls, was married in 1909 to A.J. Antelo Devereux. The groom was not particularly wealthy but came from a distinguished lineage. His ancestors included two colonial mayors of Philadelphia, Clement Plumsted and William Plumsted, both of whom served from the 1720s through the 1750s. He had graduated from Georgetown University in 1898 and went to work for the brokerage house of Cassatt and Company. The bride and groom were married by Devereux's friend, Archbishop Ryan, at Camp Hill Hall in a family-only ceremony. The rites were followed by a lavish party for several hundred guests. When the couple returned from their honeymoon, they moved into nearby Emlen House on one hundred acres, which was a wedding gift from the Van Rensselaers. The house had been built in 1750 by George Emlen and served as Washington's Headquarters during the Whitemarsh Encampment of 1777. Mrs. Van Rensselaer had John Cornell and Sons remodel the house for her daughter and new son-in-law. The couple had three children including Alexandra Van Rensselaer Devereux, who married Rodman Wanamaker. In 1910 A.J. Devereux won the prestigious National Hunt Cup. In 1914 he sold his string of polo ponies and turned to aviation. He had brief training at the Essington Aerial School and attempted to enter the French Flying Corps. Upon America's entrance into World War I, he became a captain in the AEF, the American Expeditionary Forces, whose first mission was led by General Pershing in

46

March of 1918. Devereux survived the war, but in 1920 he suffered a disastrous fall from his horse. According to the *Ambler Gazette*, Mr. Devereux made light of the incident but later had the first of a number of strokes. The family traveled as far as Europe for medical treatment, but nothing seemed to stop his deterioration. In 1924 he was moved to Friends Hospital and a guardian was appointed for him. Frances Fell Devereux quietly divorced her husband in 1924, and in 1925 married Radcliffe Cheston Jr. of Chestnut Hill. His father, Dr. Radcliffe Cheston, was one of the founders of Chestnut Hill Hospital. Frances and Radcliffe Cheston Jr. lived at Emlen House but spent part of the year at their estate, Friendfield Plantation, in Georgetown, South Carolina.

The youngest of the Fell children was christened John Gillingham Fell when he was born in 1889. Like his sisters, he was educated at home by tutors and studied abroad. As a young man John G. Fell exhibited very positive traits. He was involved with the Boy Scouts and was very interested in firefighting. He oversaw the purchase of fire equipment for the estate, organized surprise fire drills using the staff on the property and often responded to fires in the area with equipment attached to his auto. In 1910 he married Philadelphia debutante Dorothy Randolph and in 1911, when he turned twenty-one, he legally changed his name to John R. Fell, 2nd. A few stories circulated about his building a mansion of his own at Camp Hill, but none was constructed. With the outbreak of World War I, Fell was commissioned first lieutenant of Troop E, formerly known as the First City Troop. In January of 1918 he was sent to France.

By 1920 the Fells were residing at 2123 Spruce Street with their three children and seven servants. Mr. Fell did not work, but he was an avid clubman known for his string of polo ponies. The couple remained married until 1923 when Dorothy sued John Fell for divorce on the grounds of constant drunkenness. Dorothy Randolph Fell later married Ogden Mills, undersecretary of the treasury under President Hoover. The Fell children lived with their mother and Ogden Mills. In 1925 John Fell married Mildred Santry, an actress, and the union lasted until 1931. At that time papers along the East Coast ran stories of his suing her for divorce on the grounds of mental cruelty and desertion.

In 1932 John Fell 2nd married a former Ziegfeld Follies girl named Martha Enderton. About a year after their wedding, the couple took an extended trip to the East Indies. Originally Colonel Anthony J. Drexel, Mr. Fell's uncle, was to have accompanied the couple on their trip but changed his mind. Soon after arriving in Solo, Java, John Fell was found dead in a hotel room on February 22, 1933. A table knife had been plunged into his chest. Martha Enderton Fell was the only other person in the room, and she claimed he had committed suicide. Mrs. Fell was too hysterical to be questioned and did not talk to the police until thirty-six hours after her husband's death. She claimed that they had a glass of beer in the bar but came back to their room to dine in private. She said:

The table was set and my husband sat down to eat. As I recall, I was at the wash-stand with my back to him. There was no thought of tragedy in my mind. Suddenly I turned toward the table. At that moment I saw him rise from his chair and stagger toward the bed. A foot or so from the bed he crumpled up and sank to the floor. I rushed to his side, and then saw for the first time that a table knife was protruding from his heart. I pulled out the knife and threw it across the room. I was terrified and terror-stricken. I shouted for help and another guest of the hotel arrived just as he died. His last words were: "It's my fault. I did it."

Mrs. Fell told the police she had no idea why he should take his own life because he had no business troubles and his married life was happy. A subsequent investigation resulted in a ruling of accidental death although members of Fell's family thought he had been murdered. Mrs. Fell never remarried and lived in Arizona until her death in 1972.

Sarah Drexel Fell Van Rensselaer remained a force in Philadelphia high society until her death at Camp Hill Hall caused by influenza on February 4, 1929. Alex Van Rensselaer continued to be a philanthropist, sportsman, patron of the arts and cherished family member until his death on July 19, 1933, at Chestnut Hill Hospital. This couple defined society for more than a quarter of a century in Philadelphia. Although the Van Rensselaers had been received by royalty and had traveled around the world, Camp Hill was the core of their family and lives. Here they married, as did their three daughters, and here they built impressive estates for two of their daughters.

The mansion was uninhabited for twelve years after the death of Alexander Van Rensselaer. For a few years beginning in 1946, the estate functioned as a military school. The house was again vacant for a few years when in 1951 the present owners, the Worldwide Evangelization for Christ International, purchased the property to be used as a base for its missionary organization.

FAIRWOLD

Courtesy of Nick Jennings.

Adjacent to Camp Hill Hall is Fairwold, the country estate of T. Craig Heberton. This mansion was designed by Philadelphia architect Wilson Eyre Jr. and built in 1888 at a cost of $20,000. Heberton, a banker and broker, enjoyed the estate with his family during part of the summer months. Since they were not here full-time and traveled extensively, they never had the influence in the area that the Van Rensselaers did. However, they were mentioned at times in the *Gazette*. In 1907 Mrs. Heberton entertained twenty-five boys and girls from Fifth and Christian Streets in Philadelphia and apparently the event was an annual one since it was mentioned in the *Gazette* in consecutive years. In 1913 Fairwold was sold to Richard and Emily Cadwalader for $65,000. Richard Cadwalader spent the summers of his youth at his father's property Stonedge on Skippack Pike. Emily Cadwalader was the granddaughter of John Augustus Roebling, designer and builder of the Brooklyn Bridge. The Cadwaladers gathered estimates for improvements to Fairwold in 1916, and renovations took place early in 1917. During World War I the Cadwaladers allowed Fairwold to be used as a convalescent center for wounded officers. A ballroom was added in 1923. Following Emily's death, Richard Cadwalader sold the estate to his real estate agent, George Gay, in 1941. The Gay family gifted part of the property to the Oreland Baptist Church, and in George Gay's will was a clause that stated the building must always be used for religious purposes.

RIDGEWOOD FARM

This estate was built by the Harrison family, whose fortune came from the sale of the Franklin Sugar Refinery. Alfred C. and Mitchell Harrison, two of the sons of the refinery founder, were instrumental in purchasing the land and erecting the buildings on the estate. The gentleman who lived at Ridgewood Farm was William Frazier Harrison, the son of Alfred C. Harrison. The date stone on the front of the building indicates it went up in 1909, but architectural records of the mansion are scarce. In September of 1911, the *Gazette* announced that Mitchell Harrison was having a new barn built near Fitzwatertown. A week later another report appeared about a gatehouse being constructed on the Harrison estate that would be situated on Camp Hill Road. In January 1912, I.D.H. Ralph of nearby Arlington estate sold a seventy-acre game preserve to William Frazier Harrison, on which Harrison had a new drive installed. The Athenaeum of Philadelphia has records of buildings on the property going up in 1911 for Alfred C. Harrison including a gardener's cottage, a pig house, a sheep house and an apple storage house. William Frazier Harrison continued his farm here, but in 1923, Alfred C. Harrison sold the estate to the Manufacturers' Club of Philadelphia for their use. Today Harrison's mansion serves as the clubhouse for the Manufacturers' Country Club in Dresher.

CHURCH HILL HALL

Calvin Pardee purchased sixty-nine acres of land near the estate of his friend John R. Fell in 1889. The property was located on Church Hill, so named because it was home to St. Thomas Episcopal Church. Pardee moved his family from the Hazleton area because he believed living in this area would be better for his children. A first house, built for the family on Walnut Lane in the Germantown section of Philadelphia, was designed by George Pearson. Pardee used Pearson to design a country house based on the Governor Langdon House located in Portsmouth, New Hampshire. The house, Church Hill Hall, was built to house the family from May to September. When a lodge was built at Lake Placid, New York, in the late 1890s, Church Hill Hall was not in use during July and August. In 1930 Calvin Pardee's daughter Olive purchased the house and lived there until her death in 1952. The house is currently owned and used by St. Thomas's Church. Nineteen members of the Pardee family are buried in the cemetery of St. Thomas's Church.

AUBREY

Edward Dale Toland earned his fortune as a partner in Erwin and Toland, a brokerage firm in Philadelphia. In 1883 he married Charlotte Graham Rush, a descendant of Benjamin Rush. In 1895 Toland had the firm of Cope and Stewardson build a large Colonial Revival house and stable on eleven acres abutting the land of Calvin Pardee. He named his estate Aubrey. The Tolands and their five children lived in Whitemarsh year-round until they had another prestigious house built in Wynnewood in 1910 by Mellor and Meigs. Edward Toland Jr. began in the banking business but later moved to Concord, New Hampshire, to become a schoolmaster at St. Paul's. In 1914 he found himself involved in the first ambulance corps in France. A fleet of ambulances had been supplied by Mrs. William K. Vanderbilt. Toland recorded his experiences, which were later published as *The Aftermath*

of Battle: With the Red Cross in France. He wrote two other non-fiction works over the next two decades. In 1930 he was still working in Concord and living with his wife and three children. The census shows that even after the Depression he had enormous wealth.

Edward's son, Robert Toland, became involved in the oil business early on. While most of his siblings remained in the Wynnewood area, he chose to move to Aubrey. The 1930 Federal Census shows him there with his wife Susan and four young children. In 1936, however, he is included in the manifest of a ship returning from Jamaica with a wife named Augustine Van Wickle Toland, a member of the Pardee family. Robert Toland predeceased his second wife, and she continued living at Aubrey until her death in 1977.

ARLINGTON

Alexander Ralph made his fortune as one of the partners of Stewart, Ralph & Company, located on Arch Street in Philadelphia. Although already wealthy, the partners achieved mega wealth when their firm was purchased by J.B. Duke of North Carolina to become part of his newly formed American Tobacco Company in 1890. Ralph bought 115 acres from Jonathan Shaffer in the Camp Hill area in 1883 for $24,000. This section of Camp Hill actually lies in Springfield Township. While nothing has been found to indicate why Ralph built Arlington in Camp Hill, most likely the existing estates increased the desirability of the Whitemarsh Valley. The Pennsylvania Historical and Museum Commission records indicate the Queen Anne mansion was built in 1885. The structure was constructed of light chocolate colored stone and sat on landscaped grounds. The property passed to his only son, Irene Dupont Hendrickson Ralph, who lived there until 1912. His name indicates a connection to the Duponts of Delaware, but so far none has been found. I.D.H. Ralph was married twice. He and his first wife had two daughters, Eleanor (who married Captain Masturzi of the Italian Army) and Caroline (who was first married to Durant Hanson, and after her divorce from Hanson, to Dr. William A. Baker). Ralph's second wife, Genevieve, was eighteen years his junior and gave him one daughter, also named Genevieve. The couple was married less than five years when Ralph's health began to fail. According to the *Ambler Gazette*, Ralph contracted pneumonia and went to his daughter's home in Tucson, hoping to recover. He died less than a week later on February 17, 1912. He left his wife Genevieve $100,000 but left the rest invested and in trust for his three daughters. Although still in her thirties, Mrs. Ralph never remarried. Arlington was sold in 1923 to J. Franklin Meehan of the Edgehill Golf Club for $115,000 and is currently known as the Sandy Run Golf Club. Arlington was demolished in 1954 and replaced with a modern structure.

MERRIENOOK

In 1888 John M. Kennedy Jr. made his first purchase of land in Upper Dublin Township. Kennedy had started out by founding Kennedy, Willing, and Company, saddlery and hardware, and was about to embark on a forty-year career in real estate. The *Gazette* described his Merrienook estate in Fort Washington as a summer retreat. The barn on the property burned twice, and in 1904 architect Addison Hutton was hired by Kennedy's son Frederick to design a stable. There is no architect of record for the main house. Three additional houses were built on Kennedy land during the first decade of the twentieth century for three of his daughters. Current owners of 400 Orchard Lane have the original blueprints, which show that the architect was Frank A. Rommel. The plans were drawn for Edward R. Jones, husband of Kennedy's daughter, Carmita. Across Orchard Lane at 403 is Thendara, which was constructed for Bertha Kennedy Bartlett and her husband, North Emory Bartlett. A third house at 385 Ambler Road was erected about the same time reputedly for a third daughter, Emelie Kennedy Shannon. The similarities of these houses indicate that they may also be Rommel designs. A fourth daughter married Richard V. Mattison Jr. and lived in Ambler.

Kennedy's real estate office was located in the Drexel Building in Philadelphia. In addition to his numerous real estate transactions, he was involved in developing three areas of Fort Washington. In the Heights, Kennedy had houses built at 408 and 410 Summit Avenue. In 1922 he planned to build twenty houses of concrete block on Highland Avenue near Pinetown Road. Since only one house of this description exists at that intersection, the idea obviously never caught on. In 1927 Kennedy planned to build twenty houses on land near Bethlehem Pike and Pennsylvania Avenue. Before going to Sheriff sale seven houses were completed, but the remaining houses were never built. The street was later named Hollywood Road, and those same seven houses remain. The stone house at the corner of Hollywood Road and Bethlehem Pike predates the development and was built in 1908 by Frederick B.R. Unger, son of Henry Unger, who lived nearby on Morris Road.

HEDGEROWS

Gustave A. Kuemmerle was the business partner of George Bodenstein. The Kuemmerle family spent their summers at their property on Summit Avenue and Township Line Road (now Pennsylvania Avenue). His son, Gustave C. Kuemmerle, married Meta Goodrich, whose family farmed the land where the couple built their Tudor-style mansion, Hedgerows, at 528 Fort Washington Avenue. The mansion was built with Chestnut Hill stone in 1912. This property once extended to the boundaries of Dr. Mattison's land but has been significantly reduced in size by modern development, including Route 309. When Kuemmerle died, most of his estate was left to the University of Pennsylvania, from which he graduated in 1898. The university chose to use the money to endow a professorship in the mathematics department, which is now known as the Gustave C. Kuemmerle chair.

One of the best-known estates in the Ambler section of Upper Dublin Township was Dr. R.V. Mattison's Lindenwold. Since so many authors have covered the subject, we have chosen not to include the estate in this book.

This early photograph of 213 Summit Avenue shows the house with a porch, which has since been removed. *Courtesy of Adeline Cooper.*

4

THE BOOM YEARS
OF THE HEIGHTS
1885–1910

The majority of Fort Washington Heights was constructed between 1885 and 1910. Early houses were built in the Carpenter Gothic style, followed shortly by Second Empire. By 1888 the Queen Anne style invaded the neighborhood and continued into the new century. The last style to have a presence was Colonial Revival, appearing after 1895. Most of the houses were built of stone and frame construction. The Vansant stone quarry, located off Fort Washington Avenue, and Knipe lumberyard, along Pennsylvania Avenue, provided builders with the needed materials. In 1907 the *Gazette* referred to Fort Washington as "quite city-like" because most houses had gas, electric and water service. People without utilities in their houses were called "back numbers" or "moss backs."

The builders of some of the houses in the Heights were identified in the *Ambler Gazette*. A significant builder, Edmund G. Ford, moved to Fort Washington after he married. He built at least eight houses, the most impressive at 223 Madison Avenue for George Bodenstein. Many of Ford's houses were built on land purchased from A.H. and George Reed of Philadelphia. The Reeds were the sons of clothier Jacob Reed. Serving as president of the Ambler Building and Loan Association and vice-president and council member of the Fort Washington Heights Improvement Association, Ford was an important citizen in the neighborhood at the turn of the century. Since there is no architect of record for many of his houses, it may be fair to give Ford credit for being more than just a builder. Many houses of the period were constructed without the use of an architect. Mr. Ford died in 1908, and Mrs. Ford died in 1914. They were survived by their six sons: Edmund, Earl, Arthur, Lorin, Raymond and Albert.

Another builder, Daniel Sperry, built at least eight houses and a church in the Heights. He built the house at 404 Summit Avenue and lived there from 1895–1906. During part of this time period, he maintained an address in the city of Philadelphia and may have used the house on Summit Avenue while doing other construction in the neighborhood or perhaps as a summer residence. The Trinity Lutheran Church at 235 Summit Avenue, erected in 1897, may be his most significant project in the neighborhood. He built the

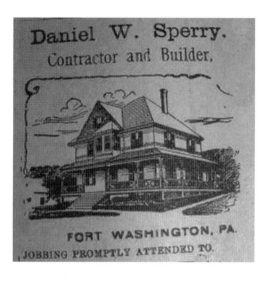

Advertisement for builder Edmund Ford, which appeared weekly in the *Ambler Gazette.*

Advertisement for builder Daniel Sperry, which appeared in the *Ambler Gazette.*

Hoopeston store in 1903, and in 1907 Sperry built the Sheeleigh School in Ambler. When the school was demolished in 1969, the stone was used to build retaining walls on the 500 block of Summit Avenue. Sperry had numerous projects in neighboring townships. Some of his notable clients included Charles Elkins, P.A.B. Widener and Sidney Thayer. He also worked with plans from important architects of the day that included C.E. Schermerhorn, Watson K. Phillips and T. Frank Miller. In late 1901 and early 1902, the *Ambler Gazette* revealed that Sperry had begun work on a new Fort Washington train station. Slate roof, terracotta downspout, bow window and ironwork from the Pettit Iron Company of Ambler created a station worthy of the developing community. The architect was Bradford L. Gilbert of New York City, who built the first skyscraper in that city using a steel skeleton. His Tower Building stood at 50 Broadway from 1888 until 1914.

Born in Virginia in 1855, John Burl built at least four houses between 1900 and 1916. While he had no large projects, his work did contribute to the developing neighborhood. The fact that he constructed the sidewalk in front of Craig's pharmacy appeared in the December 16, 1897 issue of the *Ambler Gazette.* He purchased his first lot of ground in 1887, and his family owned the house he built there at 418 Summit Avenue until 1954. The *Gazette* often carried small items about his ability to travel in his carriage from the Heights to the Fort Side Inn in record time. While the *Gazette* often commented about Mr. Burl's activities, the fact that he was a member of the African American community in Fort Washington was rarely mentioned.

George Wallace was involved in building, buying, or selling eleven properties in the Heights. He was employed by Keasbey and Mattison and later the Wampole Company of Philadelphia. Wallace was active in the Fort Washington Heights Improvement Association

NEW FORT WASHINGTON STATION.   —Courtesy Phila. Inquirer.

This Bradford Gilbert sketch of the "new" Fort Washington Train Station appeared in a 1902 edition of the *Philadelphia Inquirer* and was reprinted in the *Ambler Gazette.*

George R. Wallace was an early twentieth century community leader. *Courtesy of Mollie Luxton, Pam Jennings and Nick Jennings.*

and served as its president and vice-president and also a contributing member of the Fort Washington Fire Company. After the first firehouse burned at 223 Summit Avenue, he purchased the land on which it had existed and donated it to the fire company for a new building, completed in 1924. He also paid to maintain the community tennis courts on the site of the present firehouse. His wife Clara was the daughter of Mary Fahringer Funk, who lived at 200 Summit Avenue, and the sister of Ulysses Grant Funk, who lived at 212 Madison Avenue. George Wallace died in 1937, but Clara survived until 1954 at which time the last Wallace property at 123–125 Fort Washington Avenue was sold.

Architectural records indicate that some structures in the Heights were professionally designed. Milton Bean of Lansdale, who had transformed Dr. Mattison's house in Ambler, designed a house for Reverend Matthias Sheeleigh at 116 Summit Avenue. In 1895 Samuel Milligan of Philadelphia created plans for the building of U.G. Funk's house at 212 Madison Avenue. Perhaps the most intriguing possibility is that Horace Trumbauer designed the house at 210 Summit Avenue. Trumbauer's ledger indicates that William G. Myers of Fort Washington purchased plans from Trumbauer in 1892 for a house. Later that year he and his wife Sallie sold their property at 208 Madison Avenue and bought the lot at 210 Summit Avenue. The following year a house was constructed there. The Bodenstein mansion at 223 Madison Avenue may look like a Trumbauer design but was actually the work of a Minneapolis firm, Keith and Company.

The most significant architect in the Fort Washington area was T. Frank Miller. Miller was born in 1863 in Cecil County, Maryland. He attended schools in Philadelphia, including Central High School, although he did not graduate from the institution. His list of projects began in 1887 and includes the William Weber Johnson and Charles Eneu Johnson property in Fort Washington at 301–303 Summit Avenue. The description below from the September 12, 1887 *Philadelphia Real Estate Record and Builders Guide* explains Miller's plan for the house:

> *T. Frank Miller, 615 Walnut Street, is preparing the plans for a pair of stone, frame and ornamental shingle houses for W.W. Johnson at Fort Washington, Pa. The houses will be two and a half stories high, with a frontage of 105 feet and a depth of 90 feet for the pair. The houses will be finished in hard woods, electric lighting, electric bells, gas machines in each, and all the latest modern sanitary appliances; tank in each house supplied by windmill located at the stables in the rear, the water to be drawn from artesian wells. Each dwelling will contain parlor, library, dining and drawing room. The hall will be square. At the side will be placed the open stairway. Alcoves ornamented with stained glass will be in the hall. The contracts have all been given out and except for the wind-mills and gas engines and the work will be under the supervision of Mr. Miller.*

In the December 26, 1887 *Philadelphia Real Estate Record and Builders Guide*, construction of the barn is detailed:

T. Frank Miller, 615 Walnut Street, has under his charge most of the architectural work done at Fort Washington, Pa. He predicts that much building will be done in the spring. Two stables are to be built at the rear of the houses now in course of construction at that place for Charles Eneu Johnson, before reported. These stables will be frame, highly ornamented. Walter's cut tin shingles will be used.

The *Guide* credits Miller with "most of the architectural work done at Fort Washington, Pa." He designed and built a house for George Hoover at 209 Summit Avenue, Edward Stillwagon at 416 Summit Avenue and Nathaniel Van Horn at 302 Summit Avenue, all in the same year. A year later he designed a cottage for W.F. Jacoby at 308 Summit Avenue and a barn for Stillwagon. In the 1890s Miller worked in areas around Fort Washington. He purchased a house at 400 Summit Avenue and most likely based there to supervise his many projects. He designed St. Paul's Reformed Church and Rectory in 1894 and in 1895 designed a store and residence for James Craig. In 1897 he was awarded the contract to build Trinity Lutheran Church. By the end of his career, Miller had completed more than one hundred and fifty projects spanning forty-two years. His buildings are located as close to Fort Washington as Ambler and Jarrettown and as far away as Kentucky.

During the twenty-five year period between 1885 and 1910, 77 percent of the Heights had been built. By 1890 the building of schools and churches were evidence that Fort Washington had become a year-round community. On October 28, 1909, the *Gazette*

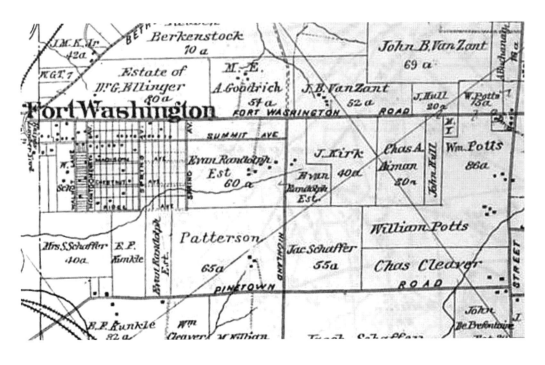

1891 map of Fort Washington Heights shows the early development of the Heights. *Courtesy of Historical Society of Fort Washington.*

commented that Ellen Rittenhouse visited the neighborhood for the first time in almost ten years and claimed that it had changed so much that she did not even recognize the place. Mrs. Rittenhouse had been the housekeeper for G.W. Stout from 1865 until 1903.

The *Ambler Gazette* updated the public weekly on the installation of utilities in the Heights. The Wissahickon Electric Company, located at 470 Bethlehem Pike, provided early power to the area. Charles Camburn, a builder in the Heights, supervised the alterations to the power plant. In 1907 a pipeline was constructed to supply the plant with oil to produce the electricity. In 1911 the Heights Improvement Association installed electric lights, seven in all, from the railroad bridge to Wissahickon Hall, which is still located at 451 Bethlehem Pike across the street from Zake's Cakes. Three companies competed for the right to supply water to residents in the Heights. North Springfield Water Company laid pipes from the Flourtown area up Bethlehem Pike. Upper Dublin Water Company laid pipes from Lindenwold Avenue down Bethlehem Pike over Montgomery Avenue to Summit Avenue. Bodenstein ran water pipes up Madison and Spring Avenues to meet the needs of residents. Gas was piped into the new neighborhood about 1905 by the North Penn Gas Company. In 1910 the company merged with the American Gas Company, and the local subsidiary was called Philadelphia Suburban Gas and Electric Company. A telephone switchboard was operating at Craig's pharmacy in 1901 and by 1902 had twenty exchanges. Trolley service to Fort Washington began on June 6, 1902, on Bethlehem Pike linking Chestnut Hill with Ambler. By November of 1909 the cars were heated!

While these "improvements" helped the neighborhood grow, not all the residents embraced the new services. When digging was to be done for telephone poles, some people stood on their lawns and chased away the workmen. In some areas wires that had been

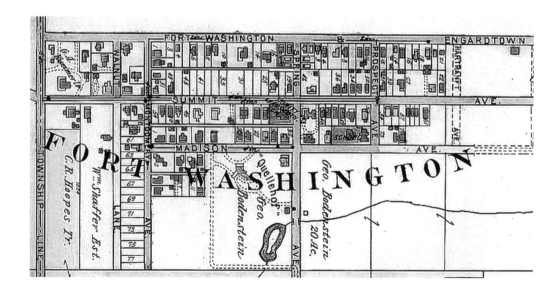

1916 map of Fort Washington Heights shows the Heights almost completely built. *Courtesy of Historical Society of Fort Washington.*

strung were stolen from the poles. People were concerned the trolleys would scare horses. Many family pets and farm animals were maimed or killed by the trolley cars. With the increase in development came an increase of thefts. Huffnagle's General Store and the post office were robbed numerous times in the first decade of the new century. The first robberies were obviously committed by people who were desperate for food, but as time progressed, the nature of the crimes changed and thieves stole jewelry, money and other valuables.

This span of time in Fort Washington saw the arrival of automobiles. As early as 1902 reports of autos in the village surfaced, and some of the wealthier residents began buying Packards and Maxwells. By 1907 the *Gazette* informed the residents of Fort Washington that on the first spring day, eighty-five cars came through the tollgate on Bethlehem Pike.

Modern improvements in transportation and utilities allowed residents more free time. Heights residents could enjoy a variety of leisure activities the new community had to offer. The Fort Washington Tennis Club had twenty members and two courts along Summit Avenue. The *Ambler Gazette* on June 30, 1910, stated that the courts were located on the site of the present firehouse, and the surface was maintained by George Wallace. A bowling alley, owned and run by Christian Sunner, existed on Bethlehem Pike just below the Clifton House property until it burned in 1906 after only fourteen months in existence. Wissahickon Hall provided the room for lectures, dances and meetings. Many local baseball teams competed, including Fort Washington, Dresher, Keasbey and Mattison, Rose Valley and Ambler. The area also had its share of popular ball players including Alonzo McCormick, Warren Dungan and Herbert Kreps. Football was not as popular early on but gained followers later. Dungan's Field, located on Bethlehem Pike and Sandy Run Creek, became the site of many activities including swimming and baseball.

Reports of the travels of Heights residents further indicate the year-round nature of the community. As early as 1897 the *Gazette* mentioned that the very wealthy sailed to Europe and the Middle and Far East. The common folk traveled also but mostly to points at the Jersey Shore. In 1901 residents were traveling to Buffalo, New York, for the Pan-American Exposition, and by 1904 many more visited the St. Louis World's Fair. The year that the least travel seemed to take place was 1898 during the Spanish-American War. The *Gazette* explained that citizens feared that the war with Spain might spread to the Atlantic Ocean, scaring people away from the coast. However, the article went on to say that very fear might prove to be a "boon to summer boarding houses inland."

The story about the fears of vacationers avoiding the Atlantic Coast proved true, and in May of 1898 the *Gazette* ran a story about the summer trade: "Summer boarders are applying every day for accommodations at Fort Side, Clifton House, and the Fort Washington Hotel. Last year places on the Heights were fairly successful, and it appears that this season, with careful management, good returns may be derived by all who can accommodate summer guests." In subsequent stories a Mrs. Davidheiser and her daughter had rented out their house and rented another building from George Wallace to open a second boarding house. Mrs. William Shaffer on Summit Avenue had summer boarders. Even Isaac Conard on the Auger Mill property on Bethlehem Pike had taken in guests.

203 Summit Avenue was one of the first houses built in the Heights. The gingerbread has been removed but the house retains its basic structure to this day. *Courtesy of Helga and Jennie Woodward.*

His speeding trotters were seen on Summit Avenue one Sunday morning taking visitors out for a tour.

One of the men who ran a boarding house in Fort Washington at the end of the nineteenth century was Charles Dennler, a furrier. He had a number of good seasons as an innkeeper at the large house at 113 Fort Washington Avenue and later at Summit House, the former boarding house of William and Caroline Shaffer that stood at the corner of Summit Avenue and Pennsylvania Avenue. After Dennler died in June of 1910, his estate was sued by a woman named Teresa Burns for one-third of the $100,000 value. She claimed to be the widow of Charles Dennler. Ms. Burns told the court that she met Dennler in 1901. In June of 1902 she willingly accompanied him to the Herald Square Hotel in New York City. She learned that he had a wife, but he told her they were separated. Dennler promised to divorce his wife and marry Burns. Since that time she said they had been living at 1218 Master Street in Philadelphia and were known as Mr. and Mrs. Burns. In 1907 and 1909 they traveled to Europe together. She said he told everyone that Burns was his wife, but they were keeping the secret because his family would object. Dennler's sister offered Burns $1,000, and the suit was settled.

5

The First Suburbanites in the Heights

Records indicate some early residents were local people moving from nearby locations. The Nash, Stout and Shaffer families had been in the area farming for years before buying their "new" houses in the Heights. The majority of the new residents came from the city of Philadelphia. Some owners had their tax bills sent to city addresses, indicating that their houses here were used as summer residences. Like George Bodenstein, who began his years here as a summer resident, some later lived here year-round. In addition to serving as primary residences, numerous houses were built as investments. Census records for 1900 indicate that some houses in the Heights were occupied by renters year-round. George Bodenstein held a significant number of rental properties until his death.

As the area developed, job opportunities were more varied. What had once been a community of farmers was now populated with laborers, railroaders and men and women of commerce. In 1900 there were more carpenters and builders in the neighborhood than any other profession. The railroad employed citizens as clerks, ticket agents and freight handlers. Some residents found employment at the nearby pharmaceutical and asbestos plant of Keasbey and Mattison. Others supplied their neighbors with goods and services as laborers, dressmakers, teachers, ministers, shoemakers and wheelwrights.

In addition to the variety of employment, residents from a variety of classes and cultures populated the neighborhood. Some residents had at least two servants and significant houses and property while others rented small structures in the Heights. Among the ethnic groups represented in the neighborhood were German, Irish, Scotch, Russian and African American.

Many neighbors were more than just neighbors. They were relatives, business associates or had been friends before moving to the Heights. Howard Spencer Jones was the brother of Julia Conover, wife of Dr. Theodore Conover. Clara Wallace was the sister of U.G. Funk. Amanda Richmond, Rebecca Shaffer and Mary Yarnall were daughters of farmer Joseph Nash. Ulysses Grant Rupp, second minister of the Trinity Lutheran Church, was married to the daughter of Matthias Sheeleigh. Peter Wade was the son-in- law of

Ambler Gazette photo of Ulysses Grant Funk retiring after fifty years as president of Fort Washington Fire Company, No. 1.

Eberhard Flues. Robert Gordon Jr., who ran the Fort Washington Hotel, was the brother of Caroline Kittson. William Potts was the brother of Laura P. Gordon, wife of Robert Gordon Jr. George Bodenstein was in the chair manufacturing business with Gustave A. Kuemmerle. They sold chairs to John Wanamaker, and Heights resident Howard Spencer Jones was the private secretary to Mr. Wanamaker. One could conclude that those who worked for the railroad knew each other. Tax records indicate that some residents of the Heights resided in close proximity to one another in Philadelphia before relocating.

The 1850 census of Upper Dublin Township lists six "Shaffer" households and relationships among these households is unclear. Two Shaffer families had a presence in the early days of the Heights. William and Caroline (Yeakle) Shaffer farmed, operated a limekiln and owned the Fort Washington Hotel. Their son, Albert, was educated at the public school in Whitemarsh and was involved with teaming, bridge building and sinking artesian wells. After their marriage Albert and Susan Shaffer owned houses on the 300 block of Fort Washington Avenue. Albert's sister Mary remained in the neighborhood after she married Fred Huffnagle, who ran the store in Masonic Hall.

Rebecca Nash married a second William Shaffer in the neighborhood. This William was the son of Lewis and Susan Shaffer who had land holdings in the area of Pennsylvania Avenue and Summit Avenue. Rebecca and William's children included Herman, who was attending Yale, the *Gazette* explained on September 22, 1898. Herman earned his BA in 1900 and went on to become a minister. Son Earl earned his Master's degree from Harvard Graduate School in 1911, and daughter Wilhelmina graduated from Bryn Mawr College in 1912. Wilhelmina taught Latin and German at Bryn Mawr.

As the community grew, so did three organizations, the first of which was Trinity Lutheran Church. On December 21, 1890, the *Gazette* disclosed that the first Sunday school session of the Trinity congregation was held in Wissahickon Hall on Bethlehem Pike. Howard Spencer Jones, Reverend Matthias Sheeleigh, Dr. Theodore Conover and Harry Young were the driving forces of the Sunday school. The first church service was held in Wissahickon Hall on February 19, 1893, and by 1897 the church was built.

Warren, Luther and Frederick Klosterman. *Courtesy of Helen Jensen.*

Fort Washington Fire Company membership in 1910 photographed at a picnic at Bodenstein's Grove. *Courtesy of Fort Washington Fire Company No. 1.*

In 1896 the Fort Washington Heights Improvement Association (FWHIA) was formed. On February 17, 1898, the *Ambler Gazette* announced that the Improvement Company would give residents signal horns for fire or disasters. The first mention of a meeting was in the *Gazette* of January 27, 1898. In February the FWHIA built a boardwalk at Madison and Spring Avenues to protect churchgoers from the mud. This was the same date the church conducted its last service in Wissahickon Hall before using the new church.

Beginning on July 11, 1903 important members of the young community met to discuss the conditions that concerned residents. They kept minutes of their meetings, and that diary is now housed at the Historical Society of Fort Washington. According to the diary, the Fort Washington Heights Improvement Association met monthly for six years to discuss and resolve such neighborhood issues as lighting (both gas and electric), roads and sidewalks (boardwalks). In January of 1913 a paragraph in the *Ambler Gazette* described the Association's resurfacing of sidewalks with crushed stone. They also organized community events such as Fourth of July celebrations. Their notes tell us that electric lights were turned on in the Heights on November 29, 1905, but were not deemed acceptable until July 24, 1906.

The Fort Washington Fire Company No. 1 started serving the community in 1908. Many of the founding members were involved with the Heights Improvement Association. These civic-minded men transferred their energy from the Improvement

The Ladies Auxiliary of the Fort Washington Fire Company. *Courtesy of Fort Washington Fire Company No. 1.*

Association to the fire company to continue to serve the community. On January 2, 1908, the *Gazette* circulated the news that men met at Wissahickon Hall to organize the volunteer group. The fire company began in an office on Summit Avenue owned by George Bodenstein. Later in 1908 a seven hundred pound steel locomotive tire, contributed by T.W. Illingworth and John McGaw, arrived from Midvale Steel to be used as an alarm. Hoopes and Townsend furnished the metal for the erection of the item. As the company grew, firefighting equipment was added with money raised from community events like picnics, oyster dinners, Saturday night dances and flea markets. As the fire company approaches its one-hundredth birthday, members of the Heights continue to serve as volunteer firefighters.

6

THE BODENSTEIN FAMILY

George Bodenstein was born in Herrent, Germany, in 1851 to Charlotte Trumper and Andrew Friedrich Bodenstein. About a year later the family left their hometown to board a ship in Bremen bound for the port of Baltimore. The *Albert* landed on July 20, 1852. The next existing records of the Bodensteins show them living in Philadelphia in 1860. George was nine, and his sister Anna was five. A.F. Bodenstein was employed as a weaver, but the census doesn't indicate where he worked.

Andrew Bodenstein had been a captain in the Prussian Army, so when the Civil War began in this country, he enlisted in the Union Army. United States military records show that Bodenstein enlisted on June 1, 1861, and was given the rank of sergeant, first class. He was assigned to Company 1 in the Twenty-seventh Infantry Regiment of Pennsylvania. During the Battle of Gettysburg, Bodenstein was captured and listed as a prisoner of war as of July 1, 1863. He died about six months later in January of 1864 of dysentery in Libby Prison.

In 1864 thirteen year old George Bodenstein began to work for Hess and Company, chair manufacturers, located at 223 South Second Street in Philadelphia. He continued there for eight years during which time he became an expert at making chairs. After being laid off by Hess, Bodenstein decided to go into business for himself, renting a building on Callowhill Street. He hired a boy named William Weaver, and he and Bodenstein made chairs all summer in 1872 entirely by hand. Their first customer, Nathan Marple, a furniture salesman, appeared in September and purchased $156 worth of goods. Other furniture salesmen followed suit including Irvins and Brothers and Grossman and Munn. Bodenstein made a point of selling to retail furniture dealers only.

During the first year, thirteen patterns were made of walnut, mostly for use in bedrooms. At the end of the year, Bodenstein entered into a partnership with John King, and their deal lasted almost five years. The business grew and larger premises were needed, so the partners bought the building next door on Callowhill Street. The machinery was moved to another building on Edward Street, and the space at 204–206 Callowhill was used as a

George Bodenstein. *Courtesy of Beatrice Bodenstein.*

warehouse. Soon the Edward Street building proved too small, and Bodenstein and King acquired space on North Laurence Street and North Second Street. Their partnership was dissolved by mutual consent in the fall of 1877.

George Bodenstein married Margaret Beatty in August of 1872 and started a family. Charlotte, named after Bodenstein's mother, was born in 1873. Another daughter, Ella, arrived in 1875, and George Jr. was born in 1876. By 1878, the couple welcomed Emma to the family, and son William made a total of five children by the end of 1880. The family resided at 2124 North Second Street, and the household included many boarders in their teens and twenties who were employed in the chair business. Emma seems to have died in infancy, and Margaret Beatty Bodenstein also passed away, perhaps from complications after the birth of William.

George Bodenstein married Elizabeth Hartranft on June 26, 1883, and they had three children, Paul in 1884, Helen in 1889 and Elizabeth in 1894. Bodenstein's granddaughter

Elizabeth Hartranft Bodenstein. *Courtesy of Beatrice Bodenstein.*

Beatrice said that Elizabeth Hartranft Bodenstein never differentiated among the children and loved each of the seven as though they were her own.

Meanwhile George Bodenstein's business continued to flourish. He tried his hand at novelties but soon returned to the chair business. At this time he met Gustave A. Kuemmerle, and on February 8, 1881, the two entered into a partnership that became a corporation in 1903. Kuemmerle bought the property along Pennsylvania Avenue between Summit Avenue and Fort Washington Avenue where Friendly's and the Abington Bank now stand. He may have lived in the existing house that once belonged to Rebecca Nash Shaffer. After his death the house and the chair business passed to his only son, Gustave C. Kuemmerle.

On May 27, 1887, George Bodenstein purchased a summer house from William Livezey at 123 Summit Avenue in Fort Washington. Less than ten years later, on January 13, 1896, Bodenstein purchased a few lots from Phillip and Carrie Arnold. He hired the firm of Keith and Company of Minneapolis, Minnesota, to design a two-story building. The *Ambler Gazette* stated in an article after the mansion was almost completed that the plans for the building were "altered and enlarged and improved upon by Mr. Bodenstein while the details were worked out by Mr. [E.G.] Ford." The actual construction took more than six years, but the family finally took up residence in 1903. Excavation for a lake began in 1904, and the lake was filled in 1905. Boating was a major source of entertainment for the family during the summer months. Bodenstein also had an icehouse built in November 1905 that could hold two hundred tons of ice. The concrete sidewalks around the mansion were not installed until 1913.

While the house was being built, Bodenstein purchased an additional forty lots from the Arnold family as well as surrounding properties from neighbors Anna Shaffer, Henry and Catherine Klosterman and Eugene and Emma Linnard. By 1901 his land holdings included most of Madison Avenue up to and across Highland Avenue. The southeast side

Label from Bodenstein chair. *Courtesy of Janet Coffman.*

Quellehof at 223 Madison Avenue. *Courtesy of Beatrice Bodenstein.*

of Madison Avenue was known as Bodenstein Grove, which later became the site of many parties and picnics. Bodenstein erected a pavilion in the grove in 1909. The eighty acres on the east side of Highland Avenue was called Highland Farm. There Mr. Bodenstein grew produce and raised livestock to feed his family. From the property on which his mansion sat, George Bodenstein pumped water to the houses on the Heights. Later Ambler Water Company bought the Bodenstein Water Company.

George Bodenstein was very generous to the community and was involved in other endeavors as well. When Trinity Lutheran Church first opened its doors on Summit Avenue in 1897, Bodenstein supplied two ornate chairs in the names of his children even though the family were members of St. Thomas's Church in Whitemarsh. He was one of the founding members of the Fort Washington Fire Company and the Fort Washington Heights Improvement Association. In addition, he was president of the Dairy Equipment and Container Company at Eighth and Spruce Streets, a life member

George Bodenstein and workers at Highland Farm on Highland and Madison Avenues. *Courtesy of Beatrice Bodenstein.*

of the Manufacturers Club, a member of the City Club and an active member of the German Society, which cared for German immigrants. He was a director of the Philadelphia Life Insurance Company, a director of the Jenkintown Bank and Trust Company and vice-president of the Ambler Building and Loan Association. He was one of the founders of the Montgomery County Firemen's Association and one of the Keystone Fire Chiefs.

As Bodenstein's business and community activities grew, so did his children. Ella Bodenstein was the first of the children to wed. She married Samuel Craig in 1897. Soon after, the couple moved to Philadelphia and ultimately to Sharon Hill. Craig was a representative for a stationary company and is listed in the 1910 Census as a salesman of envelopes. Ella Craig later gave birth to two children but neither lived long.

Her older sister Charlotte married Dr. Albert B. Donaldson in 1900. Together they had five children, Dorothea, Charlotte, Elizabeth, Eleanor and Albert Jr. The family lived on Bryn Mawr Avenue in Bala Cynwyd. Bert Donaldson passed away in 1922.

Harvesting ice from Bodenstein Lake (1911) was an enjoyable event for the local children to watch. *Courtesy of Beatrice Bodenstein.*

George Bodenstein Jr. entered the employ of his father and worked most of his life as an upholsterer in the family business. He and his wife Nellie resided on Darien Street in Philadelphia and had no children.

William Bodenstein did not follow in his father or brother's footsteps and chose instead to be a farmer. His father backed him financially in a venture to establish a poultry business. In 1917 Robert Self took over William's job of running the poultry farm. Will, as his family called him, was very bright but did not apply himself. He married Josephine Conrad, and in 1921 they had a son whom they named George for Will's father. William worked as an inspector at a powder works company and ultimately at his father's chair business.

Paul Bodenstein wanted nothing to do with the chair business; he was interested in science and photography. His father refused to pay for a college education, so Paul earned the money to attend Penn State College, from which he graduated in 1912. Paul returned home after graduation, found work as a chemist and continued to improve his photography skills. He worked for the Hercules Powder Company, which had been a part of DuPont, to develop better explosives. In 1920 he traveled to England to work with the military. There he met Mary Bettle, a woman thirteen years his junior, and fell in love with her. In 1921 she immigrated to the United States, and the two were married in August at St. Thomas's

Bodenstein family circa 1906 from right to left: *top row*: Bert Donaldson, William Bodenstein; *next to top*: Sam Craig, George Bodenstein Sr., George Bodenstein Jr.; *middle*: Paul Bodenstein, Helen Bodenstein, Elizabeth Bodenstein, Josephine Conrad Bodenstein, Nellie Gossler, Ella Bodenstein Craig, Elizabeth Hartranft Bodenstein, Charlotte Bodenstein Donaldson, Nellie Bodenstein; *children*: Bette Donaldson, Eleanor Donaldson, Dorothea Donaldson, Charlotte Donaldson. *Courtesy of Beatrice Bodenstein.*

Church in Whitemarsh. Paul's mother exclaimed at the time, "Oh, my poor Paul!" A reception followed at 223 Madison, and George Bodenstein gave the couple a dining room set as a wedding gift. They honeymooned at Lake Placid, and upon their return to the area lived on the third floor of the Bodenstein mansion in the billiard room for a few years before moving to a second floor apartment at the Wyndham Hotel in Ambler. In 1924 Mary gave birth to a daughter named Beatrice. By 1930 Paul's job took him to Virginia, and the family lived in Petersburg. Forced to look for employment elsewhere, Paul headed to Brooklyn, leaving his family in a boardinghouse. Later he went to Baltimore, and Mary and their daughter returned to live in Petersburg. Ultimately Paul and Mary separated. Beatrice Bodenstein felt that her mother was interested in joining the country club set, but Paul Bodenstein didn't dance. Beatrice lived with her mother while growing up and during her first two years of college. When her mother died, Beatrice went to Brooklyn to live with her father and finished her schooling at Barnard College.

Elizabeth and George Bodenstein. *Courtesy of Beatrice Bodenstein.*

Helen Bodenstein spent almost all of her life in Fort Washington Heights. She had rheumatic fever as a child and consequently was not very strong. Helen spent her time baking pies and sewing. She also loved to dress well, especially in furs. Her mother seems to have played a big role in her life. At one point Helen had a beau, but when her mother discovered he played cards, he did not call again. This may be the same gentleman, Mr. Harry G. Etsweiler from Tioga, referred to in the August 1, 1912 *Gazette* announcement of her engagement. Helen appears in many pictures with friends as a young woman, but she never married.

The youngest and most dramatic of the Bodensteins was Elizabeth. Her niece Beatrice called her the Blanche Dubois of the family. She can be identified in old photos by the fact that she was usually having a hard time keeping a straight face. She had a beautiful coloratura soprano voice and studied singing with Niccolo Fantigli. She appeared in *The Chocolate Soldier* in New York for a year. She also auditioned for Victor Herbert and could have traveled with him as a protégé, but her mother thought that would be improper for a young girl. Like Helen, Elizabeth never married.

George Bodenstein died on May 13, 1923, from what the *Glenside News* described as "complications from a spell of hiccoughs." Years later the family secret was revealed: George suffered from epilepsy. He left his fortune to his widow who lived another four and a half years and died on December 12, 1927. George Bodenstein's will stipulated that once his wife was gone, the money, left in a trust, was to be divided equally among the children, and if they were gone, by their children.

After Elizabeth Hartranft Bodenstein's death, her two youngest daughters moved to a smaller house at 231 Madison Avenue, another property acquired by their father in 1906 from its original owner, Howard Spencer Jones. Helen passed away in Fort Washington at the age of forty-six in 1935. George Bodenstein Jr. apparently inherited his father's epileptic condition and became childish as he aged. Beatrice Bodenstein remembers him living with Aunt Lottie in Bala Cynwyd until he died in 1942. Will died in 1944, Lottie in 1951, Ella in 1958 and Paul in 1972. The mansion remained empty from 1930 until 1946 when it was sold by George Jr.'s widow Nellie and nephew George E. Bodenstein, co-executors with the Jenkintown Bank and Trust. Subsequently, the building was divided into apartments. Elizabeth Bodenstein died in 1974, the last of the Bodensteins in Fort Washington.

7

CHRONOLOGY AND INVENTORY
OF FORT WASHINGTON HEIGHTS

1855—North Pennsylvania Railroad extends the line through Fort Washington.

1870 (ca)—Joseph Rex plans lots for William Whitall.

1873—Whitall sells land to Henry Bissinger.

1877—Bissinger sells land to Edwin Arnold. Arnold has Charles K. Aiman resurvey the land.

1879—Bissinger buys land from Daniel Nash, defaults on the deal and land reverts to Nash.

1886—George Cummings of Philadelphia buys land from Joseph Nash, son of Daniel Nash.

1887—George Bodenstein buys a summer house on Summit Avenue.

1888—Architect T. Frank Miller builds numerous houses on Summit Avenue.

1891—Two-room school opens on Madison Avenue.

1893—Trinity Lutheran Church has first service at Wissahickon Hall.

1896—Fort Washington Heights Improvement Association forms.

1897—Trinity Lutheran Church opens new church on Summit Avenue.

1901—Thomas Anshutz and Hugh Breckenridge open a summer art school.

1902—New train station built by Sperry opens.

1902—June 6, trolley service begins on Bethlehem Pike.

1903—Quellehof, residence of George Bodenstein, opens on Madison Avenue.

1917—Enlarged school opens on Madison Avenue.

1923—George Bodenstein dies.

1925—Hoopes and Townsend Steel Mill closes.

1927—Mrs. George (Elizabeth) Bodenstein dies.

The architectural styles identified in the inventory can be found in a variety of guides. The use of "vernacular" in this text refers to styles that are nondescript or a conglomeration of many styles having the attributes of no single style. Vernacular houses reflect general building design and materials in a given location. For a few of the houses, the structure was so severely changed that no determination could be made, so no style was listed. In some cases the assigning of a style is arbitrary since the house might reflect two styles.

113 FORT WASHINGTON AVENUE
Rebecca Nash
Built 1870
Architectural style: Gothic Revival

This Carpenter Gothic house was one of the first built in the Heights on land once farmed by Rebecca Nash's father, Daniel Nash. Rebecca later married William Shaffer and the property became part of a larger holding of the Shaffer family. The house was used as a summer boardinghouse run by Charles Dennler from 1878 until 1904.

117 FORT WASHINGTON AVENUE
John and Deborah Cleaver
Built ca. 1752
Architectural style: Colonial

Originally part of a nine-acre farm, this structure is the oldest in the Heights. In 1803 the Cleavers sold the property to Christopher Hocker, who in 1805 purchased and operated the Sandy Run Tavern (later Clifton House) on Bethlehem Pike. The *Gazette* divulged on October 31, 1907, that artist Violet Oakley, whose projects included the interior of the Pennsylvania State Capitol building, lived here at one time.

123–125 FORT WASHINGTON AVENUE
George Wallace
Built 1911
Architectural style: Queen Anne/Tudor
Architect: Schermerhorn and Phillips
Builder: Enoch James

This twin was originally part of land owned by Hugh Richmond and his wife, Amanda Nash Richmond. After her husband's death, Amanda Richmond sold their land (bordered by Montgomery Avenue, Fort Washington Avenue, Summit Avenue and Walnut Lane), with the exception of her house at 1009 Montgomery, to George Wallace for $3,000. He subsequently built a house, reputedly for in-laws, which was joined on all three floors by connecting doors. The house was built of local stone with slate roof and front and rear porch. Each house contained a living and dining room, kitchen, four bedrooms and a bathroom and had "gas and electric lights, steam heat, and open plumbing," claimed an article in the *Ambler Gazette* on November 3, 1910. The slate roof was put on by Arnold Aiman. In 1913 Enoch James built a barn for George Wallace. In 1916 James built a garage for Mr. Wallace. Wallace worked from an office at this location, which was the barn, garage, or a combination of these structures.

209 FORT WASHINGTON AVENUE
George Wallace
Built 1921
Architectural style: Foursquare
Barn/store
Augustus Lentz
Built 1901
Builder: Daniel W. Sperry

The structure on the rear of this property was built for August and Wilhelmina Lentz, who had a farm in Dresher and a property in Whitemarsh. The *Ambler Gazette* in 1897 indicated that the structure was to be used as a shoemaker's shop. In 1919 George Wallace purchased the property and built the Foursquare house. Ultimately the property was owned and occupied by W. Romine and Myrtle Wallace, son and daughter-in-law of George and Clara Wallace. Since the house was completed just before their wedding, the Wallaces may have intended this as a wedding gift for the couple.

211 FORT WASHINGTON AVENUE
George Wallace
Built 1897
Architectural style: Queen Anne

In 1918, Frank Ottinger of Upper Dublin purchased this house. He was a plumber who did considerable work in the Heights following Charles Kreps. The Ottinger family owned this house until 1941.

213 FORT WASHINGTON AVENUE
Samuel Houpt
Built 1876
Architectural style: Carpenter Gothic

Although built for Samuel Houpt of Abington, this house quickly changed hands. By 1881, Hugh Richmond added this house to his holdings. The structure remained in the Richmond family until 1920.

217 FORT WASHINGTON AVENUE
Fort Washington Savings Fund and Loan Association
Built 1876
Architectural style: Carpenter Gothic

This Carpenter Gothic house was probably a rental property from the time it was built until 1881 when Samuel Comly purchased the property. He sold the house to Charles and Annie Leaf in 1886. They owned a store not far away on Bethlehem Pike. While they moved from this house before

1900, the *Gazette* continued to mention their family, indicating they were still in the area. Their son Louis was a second lieutenant who gained distinction in Cuba and the Philippines during the Spanish-American War. In 1902, President Roosevelt appointed Annie Leaf the second postmistress of Fort Washington. After the death of her husband, Annie Leaf was a real estate broker involved with numerous transactions in the Heights.

223 FORT WASHINGTON AVENUE
Henry Unger
Built 1876
Architectural style: Carpenter Gothic

This Gothic cottage still sits on its three original lots. Henry Unger owned a second house at 348 Morris Road near the store he operated on Bethlehem Pike. When the store burned in 1859, he became a station agent for the railroad and later the recorder of deeds for Montgomery County. He is credited with having the Masonic Hall built in the late 1860s, according to his obituary in the *Ambler Gazette* of March 4, 1915. From 1896 H.L. Davis, who was the secretary and treasurer of Forbs Tubular Heating and Ventilating Company, and family used 223 Fort Washington Avenue as their country residence, the *Gazette* divulged on April 28, 1898. In 1902, E.G. Ford erected a bathhouse and made other improvements to this house, which were described in the March 30 edition of the *Gazette* that same year.

229 FORT WASHINGTON AVENUE
Thomas Lyons
Built 1885
Architectural style: Carpenter Gothic

This Carpenter Gothic house remained in the same family for almost seventy-five years. The third owners, Charles and Maria Kluge, sold this house to Giuseppe and Antonia Mallozzi in 1927. After their deaths, the house passed to Dominic Mallozzi and his wife Gloria. As of 2001, the Mallozzi family no longer owned the house.

233 FORT WASHINGTON AVENUE
George W. Stout
Built 1892
Architectural style: vernacular

The Stout family was long established in Upper Dublin before this house was built. George Stout was involved with quite a few properties in the neighborhood. Stout passed away in 1903 and the disposition of his properties was handled by a relative who lost them at Sheriff's sale. In 1904 the house was bought by George Bodenstein, and in 1906 the

Gazette announced that Bodenstein was having Edmund Ford build a two-story addition to this house.

235 FORT WASHINGTON AVENUE
George W. Stout
Built 1888

Built by Stout, then owned by Bodenstein, the house was next sold to William Dowler in 1919. The Dowlers owned the house until 1960.

301 AND 303 FORT WASHINGTON AVENUE
George Bodenstein
Built 1905
Architectural style: Foursquare

The land on which these two brick houses and the four brick houses on Spring Avenue sit was once owned by George Stout. Stout lost the land to the sheriff, and George Bodenstein purchased the property and had these six brick houses quickly built. The *Gazette* reported that they were rented before being completed, indicating Bodenstein had them built as an investment.

305–307 FORT WASHINGTON AVENUE (TWIN)
Daniel and Sallie Sperry
Built 1900
Builder: Daniel Sperry
Architectural style: Carpenter Gothic

In 1897 T. Frank Miller sold lots three and four of the Cummings plan to Daniel and Sallie Sperry. Miller and Sperry had recently completed building the Trinity Lutheran Church on Summit Avenue. Over the next three years, Sperry built the twin that still exists at this address on lot three. The 1900 Federal Census showed that Sperry was living at 404 Summit; therefore, this was most likely built as rental property. The water for the house was provided by wells on the property, as was the case for all the houses in the Heights prior to public utility installation. On March 17, 1898, the *Gazette* divulged that one side of this house would be occupied by Frederick Spohn, a landscape gardener.

309 FORT WASHINGTON AVENUE
Daniel and Sallie Sperry
Built 1899
Builder: Daniel Sperry
Architectural style: Queen Anne

Sperry owned this house, which was built as a rental property, until 1915.

315 FORT WASHINGTON AVENUE
Jacob Danehower
Built 1900
Builder: James Armstrong
Architectural style: Queen Anne

Like his neighbor, Ulysses Grant Funk, Mr. Danehower was on the board of directors of the Wissahickon Building and Loan Association. The local paper reported in early 1900 that this property had been rented, indicating the house was built for investment purposes.

317 FORT WASHINGTON AVENUE
Jacob Danehower
Built 1900
Builder: James Armstrong
Architectural style: Queen Anne

Just like 315 Fort Washington Avenue, this house was originally intended to be a rental property.

321 FORT WASHINGTON AVENUE
Albert and Susan Shaffer
Built 1901
Architectural style: Queen Anne

323 FORT WASHINGTON AVENUE
Albert and Susan Shaffer
Built 1890
Architectural style: Queen Anne

The Shaffers sold both 321 and 323 to George and Katherine Stong in 1902 for potential rental investment. Later in 1902 the *Ambler Gazette* revealed that the Stongs hired Edmund Ford to make improvements to one of the houses.

403 FORT WASHINGTON AVENUE
Frank Weber Jr.
Built 1902
Builder: Daniel Sperry
Architectural style: Queen Anne

Frank Weber was promoted to the job of engineer at the Hoopeston Rolling Mills in 1903, according to the October 1 edition of the *Gazette*.

By 1907 Weber served as the Upper Dublin truant officer. He was also employed by the Philadelphia Suburban Gas and Electric Company. By 1911 he was the chief of the Fort Washington Fire Company. In 1914 he was rumored to be starting a milk route. Weber was also involved with moving and hauling. Since his son was also Frank Weber and lived in Fort Washington, determining which jobs each man held is difficult. That any man would have this many job changes is quite unusual.

413–415 FORT WASHINGTON AVENUE
Charles H. Jones
Built 1927
Builder: Enoch James
Architectural style: vernacular

The construction of this property was described in the *Ambler Gazette* in the late 1920s. Its history is less clear in the later twentieth century. The property went to the sheriff and then to the Pennsylvania Restoration and Development Corporation in the late 1960s or early 1970. One possibility is that at one time a single house was later reconfigured into a twin house.

419 FORT WASHINGTON AVENUE
John Burl
Built 1900
Carpenter: William G. Myers
Architectural style: Carpenter Gothic

The *Ambler Gazette* mentioned that by February 1904 this house was wired with electricity. For the story of John Burl, see 418 Summit Avenue.

421 FORT WASHINGTON AVENUE
John Burl
Built 1916
Architectural style: craftsman

423 FORT WASHINGTON AVENUE
John Burl
Built 1916
Architectural style: vernacular

103 SUMMIT AVENUE
Enos Rich
Built 1926
Architectural style: vernacular

All the houses on the 100 block of Summit Avenue, bordered by Walnut Lane, Pennsylvania Avenue and Ridge Avenue, were built on the land once owned by William and Rebecca Nash Shaffer. Enos Rich was a plumber in Erdenheim. Most likely this house and the one at 105 Summit were built as investment properties.

105 SUMMIT AVENUE
Enos Rich
Built 1926
Architectural style: vernacular

107 SUMMIT AVENUE
"Everton Terrace"
William Shaffer
Built 1897
Frame stable built 1901
Builder: Leidy B. Heckler
Architectural style: Queen Anne

The *Ambler Gazette* of August 12, 1897, revealed that William Shaffer planned to erect three brownstones on his lot opposite Dr. Sheeleigh on Summit Avenue. His plans included using stone from the Vansant quarry. He built only one house. Rebecca Shaffer had been Rebecca Nash. This marriage represented the union of two old families from the area. The Shaffers had a frame stable erected on this property in 1901 because they had sold the back of the property, which included stables, to Hoopes and Townsend for the construction of their steel mill. As of June 23, 1904, this house was hooked up to the gas line, according to the *Gazette* of that date. In 1910 Shaffer sold Everton Terrace to Louis Kittson, whose family had been members of the community for several years. Kittson's father earned his living first with John Jacob Astor Fur Company and later with the Hudson Bay Company in the mid-nineteenth century as a fur trapper. He enlarged his fortunes establishing a steamboat and railroad line in Minnesota. Commodore Kittson at one time owned nearby Erdenheim Farm, and at the time of his death was worth $6 million. Louis Kittson was his last living child of the seventeen the Commodore fathered with three different wives. Louis was with the Hudson Bay Company from 1872 until 1883. He joined his father at Erdenheim Farm in 1883 and managed the farm after his father's death in 1888. He is credited with improving the bloodlines of American horses at this time. In 1889 he married Caroline D. Gordon and the couple had three children: Louis G. who died in infancy, Frederick Steven, born on March 3, 1890, and J. Gordon. The boys attended school in Canada.

109 Summit Avenue
William Lightkep
Built 1916
Roofer: Arnold Aiman
Interior carpentry work: Enoch James
Architectural style: Colonial Revival

The stone blocks used to build this house came from Sellersville, distinguishing it from other stone houses in the neighborhood. The Lightkep family were longtime residents of the Dresher area of the township. This house stayed in the family until 1967.

116 Summit Avenue
"Friedenheim"
Matthias Sheeleigh
Built 1890
Architect: Milton Bean
Architectural style: Queen Anne

The same architect who transformed "Lindenwold," house of Dr. R.V. Mattison, into a Scottish castle designed this impressive house. Matthias Sheeleigh was an important minister in the Lutheran Church. At the time of construction, he served as minister for the Zion Lutheran Church in Whitemarsh and the Upper Dublin Lutheran Church on Susquehanna Road. He served as president of the Fort Washington Evangelical Lutheran Sunday School that met at Wissahickon Hall beginning in

1890. Sheeleigh was a force in the establishment and building of Trinity Lutheran Church on Summit Avenue but did not wish to be pastor of a third church. Dr. Sheeleigh died in 1900, and the house remained in the family until 1913, when Wesley Stone bought the property and hired Enoch James to make improvements.

119–121 SUMMIT AVENUE
Samuel Phipps
Built 1889
Architectural style: Queen Anne

On March 31, 1898 the Reverend L.B. Hafer moved into this house. He was the second minister of the newly constructed Trinity Lutheran Church. The Phipps family retained ownership of the house and were active members of the church. Mr. Phipps was a cobbler, the *Gazette* revealed on April 23, 1905. The paper also claimed that at one time a shoemaking shop was located at this address. In August of 1908, the *Gazette* reported that this house was connected to the lines of the North Springfield Water Company.

122 SUMMIT AVENUE
George Shriver
Built 1912
Architectural style: Colonial Revival
Builder: Enoch James
Stonemason: William Lightkep
Plasterer: Albert Shook

Shriver purchased land from George Wallace that had belonged to Amanda Richmond. Mrs. Richmond, who owned the corner store, stipulated that any building on the lot could not include a store or barn. Perhaps this was her way of reducing the competition in the neighborhood. The stable in the rear of the house also went up in 1912. A piece in the *Ambler Gazette* confirmed that the building on the property was completed in May of that year. The Shrivers were very active at St. Paul's Reformed Church on Bethlehem Pike.

123 SUMMIT AVENUE
William D. Livezey
Built 1873
Architectural style: vernacular

This was the first house built on Summit Avenue. Livezey lived here until 1887 when he sold to George Bodenstein. Bodenstein used this as a summer house until 1900 when the family moved to the

Heights full time. Bodenstein was able to monitor the construction of Quellehof while living in this house. Louis Whitcomb and family moved into this house in May of 1907. He was an active real estate agent in the Heights whose family had lived in the Fort Washington area for decades.

124 SUMMIT AVENUE
Hugh Richmond
Built 1897
Architectural style: Dutch Colonial Revival
Builder: Daniel W. Sperry

This property was originally built to be a store. Hugh Richmond was a Scottish immigrant who married Amanda Nash and bought a large block of land from Arnold in 1884 that had been part of the Nash farm. The *Gazette* commented in September of 1897 that the store at the corner of Summit and Montgomery Avenues was nearing completion. A store operated at this location well into the twentieth century. Richmond never ran the store himself but rented to others. In 1898, the store was rented to a S.F. Atkinson of Clayton, New Jersey, who had a delivery wagon. In 1904 the *Ambler Gazette* commented that a drinking fountain was located outside the store for the pleasure of those passing by. A trough was included for the horses. Enoch James erected a new barn on this property in 1908 and enlarged the store. A subsequent *Gazette* article indicated that the front room was extended to the street line, a bulk window was added and so was a corrugated awning. Walter Fallows succeeded Charles Williard in operating the store in 1914. After Mrs. Richmond's death, the store property was sold to then-proprietor Battersby for $4,750.

200 SUMMIT AVENUE
Mary A. Funk
Built 1887
Architectural style: Second Empire

Mary Fahringer Funk was the mother of U.G. Funk and Clara Funk Wallace. The 1880 census indicates that Mrs. Funk and her children lived in the Whitemarsh section of Fort Washington before moving to the Heights. This house was owned by the Allen Craig family from 1909 until 1941.

203 SUMMIT AVENUE
Joseph Rex
Built 1876
Architectural style: Gothic Revival
Builder: George G. Davis
Plasterer: William J. Scheetz

This was the second house built on Summit Avenue. Rex was the surveyor who drew the plans for Arnold's subdivision of the farmland. The Woodward family has occupied this house since 1937. The information about the owner, builder and plasterer was found on a board dated 1876 found by the current owner in 1966.

204 SUMMIT AVENUE
William Ott
Built 1889
Architectural style: Gothic Revival

William Ott purchased this property from Edwin Arnold in 1884 and the house remained in the Ott family until 1922.

205–207 SUMMIT AVENUE (TWIN)
Alice Spielman
Built 1909
Architectural style: Queen Anne
Builder: Enoch James

The *Ambler Gazette* on October 29, 1908, reported that Enoch James was building this double house for Mrs. Besore. Tax records indicate the original owner was Alice Spielman. Mrs. Lillian S. Besore was an Upper Dublin teacher and the sister of Alice Spielman.

208 SUMMIT AVENUE
Nathaniel Dickey
Built 1897
Architectural style: Queen Anne

Nathaniel Dickey, an Irish immigrant, was a partner in the carpet business Dickey and McMaster, located in Philadelphia. He built this house as his year-round residence and was very involved with the Fort Washington Heights Improvement Association and the Fort Washington Fire Company No. 1. He was also the first president of the Fort Washington Building and Loan Association. In 1904 the *Ambler Gazette* commented that Edmund Ford added a port-cochere and a bay window to this house.

Since Dickey was an important and active community member, he and his family received a lot of local press. In 1906 James Dickey attended Lafayette College and Nathaniel Dickey Jr. attended Drexel Institute. Dickey's daughter married W. Allen Moore, who had a harness shop in the area. In 1906, they moved to California hoping that Moore's health would improve, but he died soon after at the age of thirty-three. Nathaniel Dickey moved to Pasadena, California, with the rest of his family after the death of his wife and lived there until his death in 1915.

209 SUMMIT AVENUE
George Hoover
Built 1888
Architect: T. Frank Miller
Architectural style: Queen Anne

George Hoover owned 209 Summit Avenue for just two years when he sold the property to George Wallace, who sold it to Peter Wade. Wade was from Scotland and worked as a dyer in the local textile mill located on Morris Road. Wade married Natalia Flues, the daughter of his employer, Eberhard Flues. Their son, P. Ernest Wade, graduated from the University of Pennsylvania with a degree in engineering. From 1947 until 1994 the house was owned by Otto Prinz, well-known photographer with the *Philadelphia Inquirer*.

210 SUMMIT AVENUE
William G. Myers
Built 1893
Builder: William G. Myers
Architectural style: Queen Anne
Architect: Horace Trumbauer

After completing the house at 208 Madison, Myers and his wife Sallie bought a double lot on Summit Avenue in 1892 from George Wallace. Myers had purchased architectural plans from Horace Trumbauer the same year, and the house at 210 Summit was completed in 1893. Myers traded the house with Charles Halberstadt for ten acres of land in Chalfont and left the neighborhood in 1899. The most notable resident of this house was Dr. Theodore Conover, who served the needs of the community for many years and was an important member of the Trinity Lutheran Church. Dr. Theodore Conover moved from another house in the Heights to rent this location. Residents of the neighborhood today recall that Dr. Conover's office was in this location. The house was sold to his son, E. Russell Conover, in 1910. E. Russell Conover was connected to the S.S. White Dental Company in Philadelphia.

213 SUMMIT AVENUE
William and Amanda Garner
Built 1894
Architectural style: Queen Anne

Amanda Garner was the daughter of Jesse and Mary Ann Shay in the neighborhood. The Garners' daughter married Frank Angeny. The couple lived in the area for many years. In 1920 Sarah Whitcomb purchased the house. She left her house to her daughter Belle Hook, widow of Walter Hook, who served as chief of Fort Washington Fire Company No. 1 from 1913–1915, 1918–1922 and 1923–1927. Mr. Hook may have had another term as chief, but he died unexpectedly in 1927.

217 SUMMIT AVENUE
William Arbuckle
Built 1893
Architectural style: Queen Anne

Arbuckle was a clerk with the Pennsylvania Railroad. His son Jesse got into the coal and lumber business in the area when he and Robert Gordon purchased Samuel Yeakle's coal and lumberyard in 1917 near the Fort Washington train station. Jesse later became the sole proprietor of the coal and lumberyard but by 1934 was managing the Fort Side Inn for Mrs. Green. Both William and Jesse Arbuckle were very active in the Fort Washington Heights Improvement Association and the fire company. Jesse later served as a member of the Upper Dublin School Board.

223 SUMMIT AVENUE
George Bodenstein
Built 1902: stable
Architectural style: Queen Anne

Originally this building was the office of George Wallace and later George Bodenstein. Local elections were held here in June of 1905. In 1906 according to the *Ambler Gazette*, Miss Eleanor Leaf opened a kindergarten and primary school in the office. In September of 1908 the *Gazette* disclosed that Bodenstein donated the use of his stable to the Fort Washington Fire Company. Enoch James was hired to remodel the stable to house their equipment. By 1910 the building had electric lights, water and a pay phone. In 1914 Enoch James made significant repairs to the building that included a cement floor and raising the second floor. On December 21, 1916, the structure burned to the ground, and Chief Walter Hook lost his upholstery business, which was located on the upper floor.

223 SUMMIT AVENUE
Fort Washington Fire Company No. 1
Built 1924
Architectural style: Dutch Colonial Revival
Builder: Enoch James
Architect: Edward Parmiter

Between 1916 and the opening of the new firehouse, equipment was stored in a rented barn at 107 Summit Ave owned by Mr. Pierce. In 1922 George Wallace purchased the plot of land where the original firehouse was located for $1,000 from George Bodenstein and donated the land to the fire company.

224 SUMMIT AVENUE
Edward and Stella Parmiter
Built 1926
Architect: Edward Parmiter
Architectural style: Colonial Revival

Edward Parmiter was a chief of the Fort Washington Fire Company and designed their 1924 building.

225 SUMMIT AVENUE
Mary E. and Emma C. Mulligan
Built 1899
Builder: Daniel Sperry
Architectural style: Second Empire

The Mulligan sisters were both schoolteachers and were very active in the Ladies' Auxiliary of the Fort Washington Fire Company. By 1916 both sisters were gone, and the property became a rental.

228 SUMMIT AVENUE
George W. Stout
Built 1897
Architectural style: Queen Anne

George Stout was a stonemason who owned a number of properties in the neighborhood. Although a mason, George was elderly when this house was built, and most likely he did not do the stonework. From 1958 until 1996 this house served as the parsonage for Trinity Lutheran Church.

229–231 SUMMIT AVENUE
Charles F. Dilthey
Built 1908
Architectural style: Carpenter Gothic Revival

Elizabeth and Charles Dilthey originally came from Germany and lived in Three Tuns. He died in 1894 and she in 1916. They had seven children including Amelia Dilthey Householder, who lived at 1112 Montgomery Avenue. William J. Dilthey, son of the original owners, was a practicing architect in New York City. Deeds indicate that another son, Charles Dilthey, sold the house in 1926. However, in the history of Trinity Lutheran Church, Lois Jennings includes information from then church member Jim Schmalenberger: "During the pastorate of Pastor Whitmoyer [1945–1947] the church sexton was Rudolph Dilthey, then an old man. 'Uncle Rudy' and his brother, Charlie, lived in the twin house next door to Jeanette Mariotz…Rudy did all the work around the church." The only explanation was that, for some reason, the brothers sold the house but continued to live there.

232 SUMMIT AVENUE
Isaac White
Built 1886
Architectural style: Gothic Revival

A stonemason by trade, in 1898 Isaac White became the tollgate keeper. The *Gazette* carried a fascinating story in 1907. Isaac White's housekeeper, Lavinia Ott, was found dead in June of 1907. She was caring for Mr. White, who had suffered a stroke. Her body was discovered three days after she expired by White's daughter, Mrs. Charles Henk. The coroner claimed that Lavinia Ott had passed away due to excessive use of intoxicants and heart disease. Isaac White died in mid-July of the same year at the age of eighty-five. Charles Henk, Isaac White's son-in-law, was an engineer with the Reading Railroad. The *Gazette* revealed that in 1912 additions were made to the house including a first floor kitchen and a second floor bed and bath, and that the work was done by John B. Martin. The hallway was made wider and extended to the back. Doors to the right and left were pushed back to enlarge the vestibule.

233 SUMMIT AVENUE
Harry Michener
Built 1909
Builder: Leidy B. Heckler
Garage built 1915
Builder (Garage): Enoch James

Plumber: Charles Kreps
Architectural style: Foursquare

This present-day private residence was originally built as a store. Harry I. Michener had been in the business of provisions in Philadelphia, and in 1909, the *Gazette* announced that Mrs. Michener opened a dry goods, trimmings and notions store here. In 1914 gas was installed in the building. By 1916 the *Gazette* revealed that Harry Michener was working as an agent for the Metropolitan Life Insurance Company. The store was later owned and run by John Stalker. Leidy B. Heckler built a few houses in the Heights, but most of his work was for Dr. Mattison in Ambler.

235 SUMMIT AVENUE
Trinity Lutheran Church
Built 1897
Architect: T. Frank Miller
Builder: Daniel Sperry
Architectural style: Queen Anne

The church actually began meeting before they secured lots on which to build their church. Meeting in Wissahickon Hall on Bethlehem Pike, a committee made plans for the construction of the church in the Heights. Ellsworth Niblock of Ambler, well-known painter and decorator, was responsible for the interiors of the church, as detailed in an article in the *Gazette* on January 20, 1898.

301–303 SUMMIT AVENUE
William Weber Johnson
Charles Eneu Johnson
Built 1888
Architect: T. Frank Miller
Architectural style: Queen Anne

This unusual two-and-a-half-story frame twin house was built by Philadelphia ink manufacturer Charles Eneu Johnson, and was one of T. Frank Miller's earliest projects in the Heights. By 1898, 303 Summit Avenue was being rented by the Tiedemann family. Frank Tiedemann went to the city daily, had an office in the Bourse, and was employed by F.E. Straus and Company of New York. The *Ambler Gazette* of January 23, 1902, announced the shocking news that Tiedemann was found dead by his wife and son. Apparently he shot himself because of business problems. Mrs. Tiedemann and son, Frank Jr., moved back to Philadelphia in March. On November 19, 1903, the *Ambler Gazette* commented that E.G. Ford was to line the stable for Mr. David Grafly, who was living here. Grafly was employed by the Reading Railroad and was a member of the Heights Improvement Association and the Fort Washington Building and Loan Association. He rented this house until his death at home on March 25, 1907. In June of the same year the house was connected to the gas line. In 1914, the house was purchased by James and Julia Y. Thompson. Mr. Thompson worked for Midvale Steel. In August of 1914, the Thompsons had Charles Kreps install a heating system in the house.

302 SUMMIT AVENUE
Nathaniel Van Horn
Built 1889
Architect: T. Frank Miller
Architectural style: Queen Anne

Nathaniel and Elizabeth Van Horn had 302 Summit Avenue built as a summer house. Mr. Van Horn had been a ticket agent for the railroad and seemed to be retired during the years that he summered in the Heights. In 1906, owner John P. Phillips opened a machine shop in the building behind the house. In 1907 he became a correspondent for the *Ambler Gazette*. Marion Phillips, his sister, was the choir director at Trinity Lutheran Church. This house was connected to the gas line on January 17, 1907. In 1909 the *Gazette* reported that Mrs. Phillips, John's mother, and Marion were moving to London so that Marion could become a concert pianist, and her son, John was to look after the house. Mrs. Phillips did return to the neighborhood, but then apparently went back to England, and in 1910 John Phillips returned to Elkins, West Virginia. The Phillips sold the house in 1915.

305 SUMMIT AVENUE
Charles Camburn
Built 1903
Architectural style: Queen Anne

In 1902, the *Gazette* stated that Mr. Camburn was a school director. Mr. Camburn lived on Cold Point Road at "Camsell" in Plymouth, Whitemarsh Township. Living with him at that location were his daughter and son-in-law, Elsie Mae and George Matz. The two men were listed in the 1900 United States Census as carpenters. The fact that the family remained in Whitemarsh suggests the houses were built as rental properties. Following the deaths of the Camburns, the Matz family moved to 307 Summit Avenue. 305 Summit was purchased by George Morris in 1919 and remained in the Morris family until 1963.

307 SUMMIT AVENUE
Charles Camburn
Built 1903
Architectural style: Dutch Colonial
Charles Camburn built this house similar to his own at 305 Summit for his daughter, Elsie Mae Matz, and her husband.

308 SUMMIT AVENUE
William Jacoby
Built 1889
Architect: T. Frank Miller
Architectural style: Queen Anne
William Jacoby was a hat maker in Philadelphia who did not own this property for long, selling the same year the house was built, to Robert and Mary Jane Yarnall. The Yarnalls went on to purchase numerous houses on Summit Avenue including 311, 318 and 319. This house remained in the Yarnall family until 1922.

309 SUMMIT AVENUE
Timothy W. Illingworth
Built 1906
Builder: Edmund Ford
Architectural style: Dutch Colonial Revival
Edmund G. Ford bought a number of lots on the upper portion of the 300 block of Summit Avenue from Allen H. Reed, one of Jacob Reed's sons who took over his father's Philadelphia men's clothing business. Ford was elected vice-president of the Ambler Building and Loan Association in 1902. Original owner Timothy Illingworth was employed by Midvale Steel and in 1912 became a school director in Upper Dublin. In 1918 the property was sold to Fred Kittson, whose family owned 107 Summit Avenue. Illingworth bought a 120-acre farm near Chalfont but continued to work at Midvale Steel.

311 SUMMIT AVENUE
Charles Kreps
Built 1906
Builder: Edmund Ford
Architectural style: Dutch Colonial Revival
Charles Kreps was an important tradesman in the neighborhood as the resident plumber. He is credited with installing plumbing and gas lines in most houses in the Heights. In 1907 a stable, complete with electricity, was built on this property by Kreps' neighbor, Charles Camburn.

312 SUMMIT AVENUE
William Livezey
Built 1891
Architectural style: Queen Anne

William Livezey was involved in a furniture business in Philadelphia from which he retired in 1884. He had lived at 123 Summit Avenue before moving to this new address.

313 SUMMIT AVENUE
Edmund G. Ford
Built 1906
Builder: Edmund Ford
Architectural style: Queen Anne

Prior to the building of the house, a barn and stable was added to the property in 1901. The masonry work was done by G.W. Stout, a stonemason who lived at 228 Summit Avenue. Although Edmund Ford built many houses in the Heights, this was his house until his death on September 6, 1908. Ford's son Raymond joined the Navy in 1906. He later accompanied President Theodore Roosevelt on a trip to Panama. Mrs. Ford resided here until her death in 1914. In 1915 the house was sold to Joseph Watson Craft of Ambler. By 1916 he advertised the house for sale in the *Gazette*, indicating that he purchased the house as an investment. The house was described in 1916 as twelve rooms with a bath. A hot water heater and gas water heater were installed in the house. A laundry area and electric lights indicate the modern nature of the house.

314 SUMMIT AVENUE
Mary Ann Shay
Built 1891
Architectural style: Colonial Revival

After Mary Ann Shay's husband Jesse died in 1901, Ellen Rittenhouse of 1004 Montgomery Avenue purchased this house for her son, Harry Rittenhouse, who had charge of Hoopeston Station according to the February 28, 1901 edition of the *Ambler Gazette*. His son George worked as a clerk at the Hoopeston store. In the September 6, 1901 edition, the *Gazette* mentioned that Daniel Sperry was building a back kitchen on the house for Mr. Rittenhouse

316 SUMMIT AVENUE
Mary L. Young
Built 1891
Architectural style: Queen Anne

This house is very typical of the Queen Anne style, with a steep roof and pointed gable. The upper sashes on the second floor windows were common on Queen Anne houses. Mary Young was a widow in her sixties and lived here with her single daughter until 1913.

318 SUMMIT AVENUE
Edmund G. Ford
Built 1891
Barn and stable built 1901
Builder: Edmund G. Ford
Mason: George W. Stout
Architectural style: Queen Anne

Since this house was part of the Ford estate from 1891 until Ford's death, it was most likely built as a rental property. In 1915 Ford's widow sold it to Robert and Mary Yarnall.

319 SUMMIT AVENUE
John McGaw
Built 1907
Builder: Edmund G. Ford
Architectural style: Queen Anne

In 1909 Mr. McGaw was a member of the Upper Dublin School Board. This house was sold to Robert and Mary Yarnall in 1911. The Yarnalls owned four properties on Summit Avenue at the same time but resided here. The other three were purchased for rental income.

400 SUMMIT AVENUE
James and Sarah Packer
Built 1890
Architectural style: Dutch Colonial Revival

While T. Frank Miller did not design the house, he owned this property and resided here for a few years while he was working in the Heights and the greater Ambler area.

403 SUMMIT AVENUE
Sylvester Cassell
Built 1902
Builder: David McCrork
Architectural style: Queen Anne

Mr. Cassell was identified as being a tinsmith in the *Ambler Gazette* on September 29, 1904. On April 4, 1901, the *Gazette* said that Mr. Cassell had given the contract for the building of two brick houses to David McCrork. The house was in the Cassell family until 1958.

404 SUMMIT AVENUE
Daniel Sperry
Built 1895
Builder: Daniel Sperry
Architectural style: Queen Anne

The *Gazette* revealed that construction began in June 1901 at this house. The Sperrys sold the house in 1906 and moved to Abington. The Coombs family bought the property in 1920 and for a time operated a machine shop behind the house. Eighty-five years later, the Coombs family still owns this property.

405 SUMMIT AVENUE
Sylvester Cassell
Built 1902
Builder: David McCrork
Architectural style: Queen Anne

407–409 SUMMIT AVENUE
Sylvester Cassell
Built 1906
Builder: David McCrork
Architectural style: Dutch Colonial

The *Ambler Gazette* made public the fact on May 4, 1905, that McCrork would build two brick houses with eight rooms each, three stories and a mansard roof. Perhaps he changed his mind about the roof since no mansard roof exists. Like the other Cassell properties, these rental properties remained in the family until 1956.

408 SUMMIT AVENUE
John M. Kennedy Jr.
Built 1925
Architectural style: Craftsman
Builder: Richard Jones
Built as a rental property, this house remained in the Kennedy estate until 1941.

410 SUMMIT AVENUE
John M. Kennedy Jr.
Built 1925
Builder: Richard Jones
Architectural style: Craftsman
Built as a rental property, this house remained in the Kennedy estate until 1933.

412 SUMMIT AVENUE
Isaac Jordan
Built 1922
Architectural style: Foursquare
Builder: Brown
Isaac Jordan was a member of the African American population of Fort Washington. He was noted as a live-in coachman in the neighborhood in the 1910 census. How remarkable that he could afford to buy land and build a house in 1916.

413 SUMMIT AVENUE
Harry Claville
Built 1916
Builder: Enoch James
Architectural style: Foursquare
In 1916 the *Gazette* reported that this house was rented to Phillip Bytheway. His wife Julia went on to be a memorable teacher and administrator at the Fort Washington School. Claville sold the house to the Bytheways in 1920, and they remained there until 1941.

415 SUMMIT AVENUE
Mary Ann Claville
Built 1916
Builder: Enoch James
Architectural style: Foursquare

416 SUMMIT AVENUE
Edward Stillwagon Jr.
Built 1888
Architect: T. Frank Miller
Architectural style: Queen Anne

Living in this house were Edward Stillwagon Jr., his wife Ella Louise, his daughter Margaret, his mother Sarah and sisters May, Lottie and Kate. Lottie ran a school in the house according to a report in the *Ambler Gazette* on September 22, 1898. In a later edition on June 20, 1901 the *Gazette* indicated that the family left for Falmouth, Massachusetts, in the summer and rented their house in the Heights. Stillwagon ran an ad in the *Gazette* describing himself as a clock and watchmaker who sold his products at Plumly's Store in Ambler. In 1945 the house was purchased by the Wiley family and saved from certain destruction. Members of the family inhabit the house today, some sixty years later.

417 SUMMIT AVENUE
Enoch James
Built 1916
Builder: Enoch James
Architectural style: Foursquare

418 SUMMIT AVENUE
John Burl
Built 1894
Builder: John Burl
Architectural style: Gothic Revival

In addition to building houses in the Heights, John Burl served the community in other ways. He delivered mail from Fort Washington to Whitemarsh and Flourtown. The early streetlights in the Heights were powered with gas, and Mr. Burl was in charge of their lighting and maintenance, explained the *Gazette* on July 21, 1898. In 1904 John Burl was on the board of the Fort

Washington Building and Loan Association. His son, John Burl Jr., planned to build greenhouses opposite the school to grow pansies that he arranged to sell in Philadelphia. Mrs. John Burl Jr. worked at Dungan's. Mr. Burl's niece, Osceola Burl, died of the grippe in 1916. At that time the *Gazette* commented that she had graduated from Upper Dublin Schools, attended Howard University and majored in pedagogy (teaching). The article went on to say that she "taught for ten years at the Gay Street School for colored children in West Chester." As of the March 21, 1907 issue of the local paper, this house had electric service. Mr. Burl, or Burrell as he was later called when mentioned in the *Gazette*, seemed to be the most prosperous member of the African American community in Fort Washington.

419 SUMMIT AVENUE
Harry and Emma Baker
Built 1907
Builder: Edmund G. Ford
Architectural style: Queen Anne
In July of 1906 Harry M. Baker purchased a lot from E.G. Ford, and Mr. Ford built a one-story house for him. However, on July 24, 1907, the *Gazette* described the alterations that Mr. Ford was making to the Baker house. A second floor was added so that the first floor could be rented. In April of 1910 the Bakers were moving to Oregon to raise fruit, the *Gazette* stated on April 7. They later returned to the neighborhood, and Harry Baker worked as an auctioneer.

204 MADISON AVENUE
George Wallace
Built 1902
Architectural style: Italianate
While George Wallace owned many houses in the Heights, this was his first house here. In 1913, he and wife Clara sold this house to Eva Pell Slater, who lived there for seven years. In 1920 she sold to Edward Cain, and the house remained in his daughter, Anne Merrill's, family until it was sold in 1999 to the present owners.

207 MADISON AVENUE
George Bodenstein
Built 1901
Architectural style: Queen Anne
This was the second property George Bodenstein owned in the neighborhood. Since he used his house on Summit Avenue as a summer residence, this house was built most likely for investment or rental reasons.

208 MADISON AVENUE
William G. Myers
Built 1889
Architectural style: Colonial Revival

William G. Myers was a carpenter. He and his wife Sallie purchased lots from Edwin Arnold, and it's possible that Myers built this house himself. In 1892 they sold the house to George Wallace and built a new house at 210 Summit Avenue on lots purchased from Wallace.

209 MADISON AVENUE
Charlotta Bodenstein
Built 1893
Architectural style: Queen Anne

Charlotta Bodenstein was the mother of George Bodenstein. He had the house built, and for some reason, put the property in his mother's name. Since she was a widow, it's most likely that she resided with the family, who still lived in the city at the time of the building of this house.

210 MADISON AVENUE
Abram A. Nash
Built 1900
Architectural style: Foursquare

In 1907, famed watercolorist Marianna Sloan purchased this property. Her 1914–15 mural dedicated to the memory of Reverend A.J. Miller hangs at St. Thomas's Church in Whitemarsh. She exhibited in numerous venues including the Art Club of Philadelphia in 1916. Sloan was one of many artists in the family. Her brother John Sloan was a graduate of the Pennsylvania Academy of the Fine Arts and a member of the Ashcan School of painting. It's possible that his connection with Hugh Breckenridge, co-director of the Darby School, brought Marianna Sloan to Fort Washington.

211 MADISON AVENUE
Mary Susan Morris
Built 1886
Architectural style: Queen Anne

In this house Mary Susan Morris had a music studio, which was the location for music lessons and concerts. She gave vocal and instrumental lessons and was especially interested in the Cheve and sight-singing method. She had been an instructor at the Sunnyside School in Ambler and the Heacock School in Wyncote. She graduated from Bucknell and had written a primer that was used at the Carnegie Institute. This information about her was published in her obituary in the *Gazette* on February 17, 1916. Later in 1916 George Bodenstein purchased this property.

212 MADISON AVENUE
Ulysses Grant Funk
Built 1895
Architect: Samuel Milligan
Architectural style: Dutch Colonial Revival

This Dutch Colonial house remained in the Funk family from the time it was built until 1965. Ulysses G. Funk was born in Cheltenham Township, educated at the Whitemarsh Public Schools and later at Pierce Business College. His career started as a bookkeeper for the Keasbey and Mattison Company in Ambler, where he quickly worked his way up to company treasurer. He further served as a director in the First National Bank of Ambler, was an elder at St. Paul's Reformed Church, was involved with the Independent Order of Odd Fellows, the Order of Independent Americans and the Fort Washington Heights Improvement Association and acted as president of the Fort Washington Fire Company from 1911 until 1949, according to Ellwood Roberts's *Biographical Annals of Montgomery County*. He also served as tax collector for Upper Dublin Township and was succeeded in that position by one of his twin daughters. Harold Funk, his son, volunteered to serve the government in 1917 and was placed at the University of Pennsylvania. Funk's twin daughters sold this home to the current owners in 1965, and they, like U.G. Funk, have been important members of Fort Washington Fire Company No. 1.

216 MADISON AVENUE
Emma K. Baker
Built 1900
Architectural style: Queen Anne

George Wallace had this house built and then sold to Harry and Emma Baker in 1900. The Bakers sold the house in 1902 and left the neighborhood. They later returned and lived at 419 Summit Avenue.

220 MADISON AVENUE
Enoch James
Built 1897
Architectural style: Queen Anne

This was probably Enoch James's first house in the neighborhood. He sold it to Mary Lower of Dreshertown in 1902.

223 MADISON AVENUE
George Bodenstein
Built 1903
Architect: Keith and Company, Minneapolis
Builder: Edmund G. Ford
Architectural style: Georgian Revival

For more information about this property and the Bodensteins, see chapter six.

224 MADISON AVENUE
George Bodenstein
Built 1902
Builder: Daniel Sperry
Architectural style: Queen Anne

From March 27, 1926, until December 5, 1958, this house served as the parsonage for Trinity Lutheran Church. This house is unusual because it is one of the few brick houses in the neighborhood.

226 MADISON AVENUE
George Bodenstein
Built 1902
Builder: Edmund G. Ford
Architectural style: Queen Anne

George Bodenstein rented quite a few of his properties. When his widow sold this one in 1925, she stipulated in the deed that she had the final say on tree-trimming rules.

228 MADISON AVENUE
Edwin Arnold
Built 1886
Architectural style: Second Empire

Edwin Arnold was a partner in the clothing business of Steppacher and Arnold in Philadelphia. In 1877 Arnold bought land below Spring Avenue from Henry Bissinger, a real estate agent, and had that land surveyed by Charles Aiman and divided into lots. Arnold continued selling lots until his death in 1894, at which time the land was willed to his brothers and sisters. In 1900 the heirs of Arnold sold the property to George Bodenstein. In 1912 the property was sold to Susan Lavinia Utt, who willed the property to her daughter, Marion Dowler. The *Gazette* reports that David McCrork built a brick garage for Mr. Dowler in 1913. The property remained in the Dowler family until 1959.

231 MADISON AVENUE
Howard Spencer Jones
Built 1886
Builder: Enoch James
Architectural style: Second Empire

Howard S. Jones was the private secretary to John Wanamaker. He was instrumental in establishing Trinity Lutheran Church. Jones and his wife remained at 231 until 1907 when they sold the house to George Bodenstein. After the deaths of George Bodenstein and his wife, their youngest daughters, Helen and Elizabeth, lived here until their deaths. In 1974, following the death of Elizabeth Bodenstein, the house left the family.

306–308 MADISON AVENUE
Charles Camburn
Built 1906
Architectural style: Colonial Revival

After Camburn died in 1914, the Bimson family bought at least one half of this house. They actually lived at 306, but whether they also owned 308 is unclear. Thomas Bimson was superintendent of Hoopeston Steel Mill until March 2, 1916, when he resigned, according to the *Gazette*. On June 25, 1914, the *Gazette* commented that Clinton G. Bimson was attending the Philadelphia College of Pharmacy.

319 MADISON AVENUE
Built 1891, 1917
Architect 1917: Watson K. Phillips
Builder 1917: William L. Hampton
Electrical work 1917: J. F. Buchman
Heating 1917: American Heating and Ventilation Company
Plumbing 1917: Frank S. Ottinger
Cost 1917 building: $31,066

The original Fort Washington School was built in 1891 and consisted of two rooms with the entrance on Madison Avenue. In 1902 it was enlarged with an addition of twenty-eight feet by forty feet, and the entrance now faced Prospect Avenue. Fifteen years later it was enlarged again to its current size.

400 MADISON AVENUE
Luther Klosterman
Built 1922
Builder: Enoch James
Architectural style: Foursquare

This house was one of the later ones built in the Heights. The original owner of this house grew up in the Heights when his family lived at 1200 Montgomery Avenue. Luther's father, Frederick, worked in the auditing department of the Reading Railroad at the Reading Terminal office for fifty years. In 1897, Frederick Klosterman beat E.G. Ford for school director in Upper Dublin Township, the *Gazette* stated on February 25, 1897. While the family lived in the Shaffer property at 107 Summit Avenue, the *Gazette* claimed on March 31, 1898, that Frederick dabbled in the incubation of chickens and ducks. Luther married Helen Sigmund, who was the daughter of Reverend Sigmund, former pastor at Trinity Lutheran Church. The Klosterman family has owned various houses in the neighborhood, and this home remains in the family today.

404 MADISON AVENUE
Enoch James
Built 1909
Builder: Enoch James
Architectural style: Queen Anne

Enoch James was an important builder in the Heights who was well established in the area before building this house. 404 Madison remained in the James family for sixty-five years.

406 MADISON AVENUE
Morris Wert
Built 1906
Builder: Enoch James
Architectural style: Queen Anne

The *Gazette* reported that Wert bought this land from Edmund Ford and the basement was started October 5, 1905. By 1906 the family was living here, and in 1912 they sold the property to George Bodenstein.

414 MADISON AVENUE
Charles Messick
Built 1925
Architectural style: Colonial Revival

Charles Messick owned this property just four years before selling.

1002 MONTGOMERY AVENUE
Adeleane Greenwood
Built 1916
Architectural style: Foursquare

1004 MONTGOMERY AVENUE
Ellen Rittenhouse
Built 1890
Architectural style: Queen Anne
Ellen Rittenhouse was housekeeper for George W. Stout for almost forty years but owned this house for less than two years. Her son H.H. Rittenhouse lived in Fort Washington all of his life. Newberry Rittenhouse, son of H.H., had a real estate business on Bethlehem Pike.

1006 MONTGOMERY AVENUE
George Wallace
Built 1909
Architects: C.E. Schermerhorn, Watson K. Phillips
Builder: Leidy B. Heckler
Architectural style: Queen Anne

1009 MONTGOMERY AVENUE
Christopher Hocker
Built 1804
Architectural style: Colonial
This stone structure is the second oldest house in the Heights and sits on land that was owned by the Nash family and later the Richmond family. Amanda Richmond apparently was well off after her husband's death since she traveled extensively. She died in this house unexpectedly in 1922 after being asphyxiated by gas. She was seventy-six years old and left the bulk of her estate to St. Thomas's Church. The house was sold by Mrs. Richmond's executors to J. Howard Buck, superintendent of schools, for $8,150. However, a correspondent for the *Gazette* wrote, "It

is said that George Wallace is the real purchaser of the dwelling house property which adjoins his holdings here." Robert Buck verified this rumor that his father did buy the house for Mr. Wallace at his request.

1107 MONTGOMERY AVENUE
Charles and Annie Shaffer
Built 1885
Architectural style: Second Empire

Charles Shaffer was the brother of William Shaffer who lived at 107 Summit Avenue. At one time this property included a barn and chicken house. These structures were tenanted by Fred Klosterman and family. William Potteiger moved here in 1901 with his family. He was employed at Hoopes and Townsend. His son was rumored to run an oyster saloon in the former grocery store. Indoor plumbing and a cooking range were added to the house by Frank Ottinger, a local plumber, in 1916.

1112 MONTGOMERY AVENUE
Amelia Householder
Built 1888
Architectural style: Queen Anne

In 1891 the house was sold to Elizabeth and Charles Dilthey, the parents of Amelia Householder. The house was rented to the Worrell family who were year-round residents of the Heights and active at Trinity Lutheran Church. Their son, Sam K. Worrell, printed an early monthly newspaper, called the *Sentinel*.

1200 MONTGOMERY AVENUE
Josiah and Mary Bryan
Built 1891
Architectural style: Queen Anne

In March of 1904, Ida Walker sold this house to George Bodenstein. He had it partially torn down and repaired by E.G. Ford. This information, gathered from some 1904 issues of the *Ambler Gazette*, explains the unusual style of this house.

1201 MONTGOMERY AVENUE
Barbara Wink
Built 1885
Architectural style: Second Empire

In 1897 the *Gazette* mentioned that Fred Wink planted a vineyard on the property and celebrated his fifty-first birthday. He is credited with starting the movement to build the Fort Washington School, which opened in

1891. Wink died in 1901 and then the family made renovations to the house and rented it out.

1205 MONTGOMERY AVENUE
Joseph Walt
Built 1926
Architectural style: Colonial Revival

From outward appearances, this house may seem to have been built in the late eighteenth or early nineteenth century, but no such documentation has been found. The land on which the house is built was purchased in 1922 by Joseph Walt, who was a paint contractor in the area, and the house remained in the Walt family until 1963. At one time this lot was a part of the Wink estate at 1201 Montgomery. When Walt purchased the land, the deed stipulated that it be used for dwellings only, no pigs or cattle, and outbuildings had to be twenty feet from the property line.

1206 MONTGOMERY AVENUE
George Bodenstein
Built pre-1891
Architectural style: Colonial Revival

While the tax records indicate this house and the one at 1210 Montgomery Avenue were built in 1903, other evidence supports a second idea. The *Ambler Gazette* of November 13 and November 27, 1902, described how Mr. Bodenstein had moved two houses at least six hundred feet to squarely face Montgomery Avenue just below the property of Harry Walker. This account clearly refers to these two houses. On the 1891 map of the neighborhood, two houses were indicated on Chestnut Street. Since this location became part of the Bodenstein estate Quellehof in 1903, these were probably the houses that Bodenstein moved to Montgomery Avenue. With this said, the houses had to have been constructed earlier than 1903. Since these houses appear on the 1891 map on Chestnut Street, we have dated them as pre-1891.

1210 MONTGOMERY AVENUE
George Bodenstein
Built pre-1891
Architectural style: Gothic Revival

See 1206 Montgomery Avenue.

1045 WALNUT LANE
Mary Gimber
Built 1898
Architectural style: Dutch Colonial Revival

In 1907 the Kuemmerle family purchased this house while owning other properties in the neighborhood. It's difficult to say if this was their house or an investment property. It remained in the family until 1945.

1175 WALNUT LANE
William Shaffer
Built 1910
Builder: Daniel Sperry
Architectural style: Dutch Colonial

A notation in the *Gazette* came in November 1910 which may refer to this house: "William Shaffer is excavating for the cellar of a frame house 22'x28' fronting on the small alley alongside his property from Summit."

1004 SPRING AVENUE
George Bodenstein
Built 1905
Architectural style: Foursquare

Gas fixtures were added to the Spring Avenue houses in January of 1907 according to a report in the *Ambler Gazette*.

1005 SPRING AVENUE
George Bodenstein
Built 1905
Architectural style: Foursquare

In 1942 this house was purchased by Arthur Haggar and his wife Dorothy, who lived here for the rest of their lives. Art had sixty-seven years of active service with the Fort Washington Fire Company, serving as chief engineer for fifty of those years.

1006 SPRING AVENUE
George Bodenstein
Built 1905
Architectural style: Foursquare

1007 SPRING AVENUE
George Bodenstein
Built 1905
Architectural style: Foursquare

In 1918 Arthur George Haggar, chauffeur and mechanic for Richard M. Cadwalader Jr., moved into this house, which he later purchased in 1924. The Haggar family has been instrumental in the success of the Fort Washington Fire Company No. 1. Arthur George Haggar originally came from England and worked for a few years at the Seddon Garage in Flourtown. He was chief engineer for the Fort Washington Fire Company for three years. His sons, George and Art, continued his dedication to the fire company. His son George, who moved into this house and lived there until 1962, was chief of the fire company from 1954 until 1971. George was also the force behind the development and construction of the fire company's training grounds near the Burn Brae Station. He has been instrumental in keeping the history of the fire company.

1205–1208 BODEN PLACE
George Bodenstein
Built 1900
Architectural style: Victorian vernacular

This modest Carpenter Gothic house was built by George Bodenstein for his mother, Charlotte, whom he called Mutter. She apparently refused to live in the mansion because it was too grand. An article in the *Ambler Gazette* notes that Bodenstein was building a house for his mother in 1904. Either the *Gazette* was not correct in its reporting or the deed work was not correct. This house was definitely identified as Mutter's house by George Bodenstein's granddaughter.

1212 BODEN PLACE
George Bodenstein
Built 1909
Architectural style: Carpenter Gothic

This house was the residence of the caretaker for the Bodenstein estate, Mr. Zenobia. Some of the residents in the neighborhood recall playing with his children Angelina and Joseph.

1230 BIRCH LANE
George W. Stout
Built 1885
Builder: Edmund G. Ford
Architectural style: vernacular

In 1917 Enoch James constructed a frame addition to this property for George Bodenstein, according to the *Gazette*. This was the earliest and the most modest of Stout's houses in the Heights.

BUILDINGS LOST

While most of the original structures remain today in the Heights, some have been lost due to "progress." Listed below is what is known about each of these structures.

1. Summit House: Located on Township Line Road (Pennsylvania Avenue) between Engardtown Road (Fort Washington Avenue) and Summit Avenue. This large building first appeared clearly on the 1886 map, but it is difficult to tell if it's present on the 1877 map. It was most likely used as a boardinghouse for summer visitors. The property was later purchased by Gustave A. Kuemmerle and continued as a residence. In the twentieth century it was used as Merritt's Nursing Home before being torn down and replaced by a Friendly's restaurant.

2. Norman Virkler house: Built by Enoch James in 1922 for his son-in-law, this house stood on Madison Avenue where Route 309 now cuts through the neighborhood.

3. Earl Weikert house: This house was built on Summit Avenue and backed up onto the Virkler property on Madison Avenue. This house was also removed when Route 309 was created.

View showing Craig's Pharmacy, Fort Washington, Pa.

4. Craig's Pharmacy/Dr. Craig's office and business block: Located on Summit Avenue below Pennsylvania Avenue. Craig's Pharmacy was designed by architect T. Frank Miller and is pictured in an early postcard of the area. The buildings were demolished by SEPTA to make way for parking at the train station.

5. 407, 409, 411 FORT WASHINGTON AVENUE
Margaret and William Blake
Built 1891

Tracing this property is difficult. The information cited here was based on using lot numbers according to the Cummings plan as well as tax and deed information. In 1921 a brick dwelling stood at this address. It is possible that properties along this block of Fort Washington Avenue were renumbered after houses were built. In 1977 the property was sold for $7,500. There were two owners in 1985; one half sold for $100,000. This indicated the original structure was most likely replaced.

8

THE PROPERTIES OF
FORT WASHINGTON HEIGHTS

#	Street	Year	Name
230	Birch Lane	1885	Stout, George W.
1205/ 1208	Boden Place	1900	Bodenstein, George
1209/ 1212	Boden Place	1909	Bodenstein, George
113	Fort Washington Avenue	1870	Nash, Rebecca
117	Fort Washington Avenue	ca. 1752	Cleaver, John and Deborah
123, 125	Fort Washington Avenue	1911	Wallace, George
209	Fort Washington Avenue	1921	Wallace, George
211	Fort Washington Avenue	1897	Smith, Robert
213	Fort Washington Avenue	1876	Houpt, Samuel
217	Fort Washington Avenue	1876	Fort Washington Savings Fund and Loan Association
223	Fort Washington Avenue	1876	Unger, Henry
229	Fort Washington Avenue	1885	Lyons, Thomas
233	Fort Washington Avenue	1892	Stout, George W.
235	Fort Washington Avenue	1888	Stout, George W.
301	Fort Washington Avenue	1905	Bodenstein, George
303	Fort Washington Avenue	1905	Bodenstein, George
305	Fort Washington Avenue	1900	Sperry, Daniel and Sallie
307	Fort Washington Avenue	1900	Sperry, Daniel and Sallie
309	Fort Washington Avenue	1899	Sperry, Daniel and Sallie
315	Fort Washington Avenue	1900	Danehower, Jacob
317	Fort Washington Avenue	1900	Danehower, Jacob

#	Street	Year	Name
321	Fort Washington Avenue	1901	Shaffer, Albert and Susan
323	Fort Washington Avenue	1890	Shaffer, Albert and Susan
403	Fort Washington Avenue	1902	Weber, Frank Jr.
407, 409, 411	Fort Washington Avenue	1891	Blake, Margaret and William
413/415	Fort Washington Avenue	1927	Jones, Charles H.
419	Fort Washington Avenue	1900	Burl, John
421	Fort Washington Avenue	1916	Burl, John
423	Fort Washington Avenue	1916	Burl, John
204	Madison Avenue	1902	Wallace, George
207	Madison Avenue	1901	Bodenstein, George
208	Madison Avenue	1889	Meyers, William
209	Madison Avenue	1893	Bodenstein, Charlotta W.
210	Madison Avenue	1900	Nash, Abram A.
211	Madison Avenue	1886	Morris, Mary Susan
212	Madison Avenue	1895	Funk, Ulysses Grant
216	Madison Avenue	1900	Baker, Emma K.
220	Madison Avenue	1897	James, Enoch
223	Madison Avenue	1903	Bodenstein, George
224	Madison Avenue	1902	Bodenstein, George
226	Madison Avenue	1902	Bodenstein, George
228	Madison Avenue	1886	Arnold, Edwin
231	Madison Avenue	1886	Jones, Howard Spencer
306	Madison Avenue	1906	Camburn, Charles
308	Madison Avenue	1906	Camburn, Charles
319	Madison Avenue	1891/1917	Upper Dublin Township
400	Madison Avenue	1922	Klosterman, Luther
404	Madison Avenue	1909	James, Enoch
406	Madison Avenue	1906	Wert, Morris
414	Madison Avenue	1925	Messick, Charles
1002	Montgomery Avenue	1916	Greenwood, Adeleane
1004	Montgomery Avenue	1890	Rittenhouse, Ellen
1006	Montgomery Avenue	1909	Wallace, George
1009	Montgomery Avenue	1804	Hocker, Christopher
1107	Montgomery Avenue	1885	Shaffer, Charles and Annie
1112	Montgomery Avenue	1888	Householder, Amelia
1200	Montgomery Avenue	1891	Bryan, Josiah and Mary

#	Street	Year	Name
1201	Montgomery Avenue	1885	Wink, Barbara
1205	Montgomery Avenue	1926	Walt, Joseph
1206	Montgomery Avenue	Pre-1891	Bodenstein, George
1210	Montgomery Avenue	Pre-1891	Bodenstein, George
1004	Spring Avenue	1905	Bodenstein, George
1005	Spring Avenue	1905	Bodenstein, George
1006	Spring Avenue	1905	Bodenstein, George
1007	Spring Avenue	1905	Bodenstein, George
103	Summit Avenue	1926	Rich, Enos
105	Summit Avenue	1926	Rich, Enos
107	Summit Avenue	1897	Shaffer, William
109	Summit Avenue	1916	Lightkep, William
116	Summit Avenue	1890	Sheeleigh, Matthias
119–121	Summit Avenue	1889	Phipps, Samuel
122	Summit Avenue	1912	Shriver, George
123	Summit Avenue	1873	Livezey, William D.
124	Summit Avenue	1897	Richmond, Hugh
200	Summit Avenue	1887	Funk, Mary A.
203	Summit Avenue	1876	Rex, Joseph
204	Summit Avenue	1889	Ott, William
205	Summit Avenue	1909	Spielman, Alice
207	Summit Avenue	1909	Spielman, Alice
208	Summit Avenue	1897	Dickey, Nathaniel
209	Summit Avenue	1888	Hoover, George
210	Summit Avenue	1893	Meyers, William
213	Summit Avenue	1894	Garner, William and Amanda
217	Summit Avenue	1893	Arbuckle, William
223	Summit Avenue	1902/1924	Stable/stone Dutch colonial
224	Summit Avenue	1927	Parmiter, Edward and Stella
225	Summit Avenue	1899	Mulligan, Mary E and Emma C.
228	Summit Avenue	1897	Stout, George W.
229, 231	Summit Avenue	1908	Dilthey, Charles F.
232	Summit Avenue	1886	White, Isaac
233	Summit Avenue	1909	Michener, Harry
235	Summit Avenue	1897	Trinity Lutheran Church
301	Summit Avenue	1888	Johnson, William Weber
302	Summit Avenue	1889	Van Horn, Nathanial

#	Street	Year	Name
303	Summit Avenue	1888	Johnson, William Weber
305	Summit Avenue	1903	Camburn, Charles
307	Summit Avenue	1903	Camburn, Charles
308	Summit Avenue	1889	Jacoby, William
309	Summit Avenue	1906	Illingworth, Timothy W.
311	Summit Avenue	1906	Kreps, Charles
312	Summit Avenue	1891	Livezey, William
313	Summit Avenue	1906	Ford, Edmund G.
314	Summit Avenue	1891	Shay, Mary Ann
316	Summit Avenue	1891	Young, Mary L.
318	Summit Avenue	1891	Ford, Edmund G.
319	Summit Avenue	1907	McGaw, John
400	Summit Avenue	1890	Packer, James W. and Sarah
403	Summit Avenue	1902	Cassell, Sylvester
404	Summit Avenue	1895	Sperry, Daniel
405	Summit Avenue	1902	Cassell, Sylvester
407,409	Summit Avenue	1906	Cassell, Sylvester
408	Summit Avenue	1925	Kennedy, John M.
410	Summit Avenue	1925	Kennedy, John M.
412	Summit Avenue	1922	Jordan, Isaac
413	Summit Avenue	1916	Claville, Harry
415	Summit Avenue	1916	Claville, Mary Ann
416	Summit Avenue	1888	Stellwagon, Edward Jr.
417	Summit Avenue	1916	James, Enoch
418	Summit Avenue	1894	Burl, John
419	Summit Avenue	1907	Baker, Harry and Emma
1045	Walnut Lane	1898	Gimber, Mary
1175	Walnut Lane	1910	Shaffer, William

BIBLIOGRAPHY

Addison, Edward T. Jr. "A Brief History of the Clifton House." North Wales, PA, 1986.

Altemus, Eleanor Ward. *A History of the Clifton House Property*. Fort Washington, 1984.

Ambler Gazette. 1897–1934.

Ambler Gazette, "Fifty Years in Business," May 18, 1922.

Ambler Gazette, "Founder of Questers Dies, Noted in Area," January 2, 1964.

Atlas of the County of Montgomery and the State of Pennsylvania. Philadelphia: G.M. and Company, 1871.

Atlas of the North Penn Section of Montgomery County, Pa. Philadelphia: A.H Mueller, 1916.

Bean, Theodore W., ed. *History of Montgomery County, Pennsylvania*. Philadelphia: Everts & Peck, 1884.

Brandt, Francis Burke, and Henry Volkmar Gummere. *Byways and Boulevards In and About Historic Philadelphia*. Philadelphia: Corn Exchange National Bank, 1925.

A Combination Atlas Map of Montgomery County Pennsylvania. Philadelphia: J.D. Scott, 1877.

Evening Ledger, "Drexel Grandson Sues for Divorce," August 11, 1931.

Foulke, C. Pardee, and William G. Foulke. *Calvin Pardee, 1841–1923: His Family and His Enterprises*. Philadelphia: The Pardee Company, 1979.

Glenside News, "George Bodenstein Is Dead," May 15, 1923.

Griffin, Randall C. *Thomas Anshutz: Artist and Teacher*. Huntington, NY: Heckscher Museum, 1994.

Heineman, Heinze J. "The Whitemarsh Triangle: A Study of a Small Area of Land." Fort Washington, PA, July 1989. Collection of Historical Society of Fort Washington.

Hilton, Suzanne. *Yesterday's People: The Upper Dublin Story*. Philadelphia: The Winchell Company, 1975.

Historical Society of Fort Washington. *Fort Washington and Upper Dublin*. Charleston, SC: Arcadia Publishing, 2004.

Hough, Dr. Mary P.H. *Early History of Ambler*. N.p.: IMS America LTD, 1936.

Indiana Evening Gazette, "Polo Star Kills Self in Java," February 23, 1933.

Jennings, Lois. *A 100 Year History of Trinity Evangelical Lutheran Church, Fort Washington, Pennsylvania, 1894–1994*. May 1995.

Jennings, Ralph N. Jr. et al. *Fort Washington Fire Company No. 1, Fort Washington, Pennsylvania, 1908 to 1976*. December 1981.

King, Moses. *Philadelphia and Notable Philadelphians*. New York: Blanchard, 1901.

Minutes of Fort Washington Heights Improvement Association, 1903–1908.

The North American, "Students at Summer Art School Close to Nature," July 25, 1909.

Philadelphia Inquirer. "A.J.A. Devereux to Be Buried Today," December 19. 1940.

Philadelphia Inquirer, "John R. Fell Is Stabbed to Death in Java Hotel," February 23, 1933.

Philadelphia Inquirer, "Richest Widow in Town Weds," January 28, 1898.

The Philadelphia Real Estate Record and Builders' Guide. 1887–1897. Accessed from the Collection of the Athenaeum of Philadelphia.

Pennsylvania Historical and Museum Commission. "PHMC Cultural Database."

A Property Atlas of Montgomery County Pennsylvania. Philadelphia: J.L. Smith Company, 1893.

Roberts, Ellwood, ed. *Biographical Annals of Montgomery County Pennsylvania*. New York: T.S. Benham & Company and the Lewis Publishing Company, 1904.

Schwager, Michael J., and Jean Barth Toll, eds. *Montgomery County: The Second Hundred Years*. Norristown, PA: Montgomery County Federation of Historical Societies, 1983.

St. John, Bruce. *John Sloan's New York Scene*. New York: Harper & Row, 1965.

Supplement to the Bulletin of the National Association of Watch and Clock Collectors, Inc., Columbia, Pennsylvania, summer 1966.

Tatman, Sandra, and Roger Moss. *Biographical Dictionary of Philadelphia Architects: 1700–1930.* Boston: G.K. Hall and Company, 1984.

U.S. Census, 1850–1930, population schedule, Upper Dublin, Montgomery County, Pennsylvania; digital image, http://www.ancestry.com.

Wiley, Samuel T. *Biographical and Portrait Cyclopedia of Montgomery County.* Philadelphia: Biographical Publishing Co., 1895.

Yeakle, William A. "Whitemarsh." *Historical Sketches.* Norristown, PA: Historical Society of Montgomery County, 1895.

ABOUT THE AUTHORS

Trudy and Lew Keen began their passion for Victoriana after a 1981 visit to Cape May, New Jersey. Twenty-five years later the couple has extensive collections of antiques and memorabilia from the era. Moving to an 1888 Queen Anne house in Fort Washington fostered an interest in local history. Trudy's interest in genealogy coupled with Lew's interest in historic preservation has led the couple into researching, writing and presenting the stories of this fascinating time period.